Convection Oven Cookbook for Beginners

Convection Oven Recipes

With Essential Cooking Techniques To Roast, Grill And Bake In The Convection Oven

Kimberly Braden

Copyright © 2020 Kimberly Braden

All rights reserved. No part of this publication may be reproduced, distributed, or transmitted in any form or by any means, including photocopying, recording, or other electronic or mechanical methods, without the prior written permission of the publisher, except in the case of brief quotations embodied in critical reviews and certain other noncommercial uses permitted by copyright law.

ISBN: 9798637124022

Limit of Liability

The information in this book is solely for informational purposes, not as a medical instruction to replace the advice of your physician or as a replacement for any treatment prescribed by your physician. The author and publisher do not take responsibility for any possible consequences from any treatment, procedure, exercise, dietary modification, action or application of medication which results from reading or following the information contained in this book.

If you are ill or suspect that you have a medical problem, we strongly encourage you to consult your medical, health, or other competent professional before adopting any of the suggestions in this book or drawing inferences from it.

This book and the author's opinions are solely for informational and educational purposes. The author specifically disclaims all responsibility for any liability, loss, or risk, personal or otherwise which is incurred as a consequence, directly or indirectly, of the use and application of any of the contents of this book.

DEDICATION

To All who desire to live And Eat Healthy

TABLE OF CONTENT

INTRODUCTION 1

    Understanding The Convection Oven 1

    What is Convection Oven 1

    What is Convection Setting? 1

Does Convection Oven Cook Faster Than A Conventional Oven? 2

    Tips For Cooking With The Convection Oven 2

    How To Use Different Settings On Convection Oven .. 4

    What Can You Cook In The Convection Oven? 5

    How To Convert Traditional Oven Recipes For Convection Oven 5

BREAKFAST RECIPES 7

    Ham-Cheese Scallions Omelet Frittatas 8

    Cinnamon French Toast 9

    Falafel Tzatziki Sauce Tacos 10

    Baby Spinach Scallions Casserole Frittata 11

    Convection Crumbled Bacon With Sweet Potatoes .. 12

    Oatmeal Bars With Blueberries Pumpkin 13

    Veggie Omelet 14

    Sausage Cheese Casserole 15

Convection Oven Omelet 16

Early Morning Hash 18

LUNCH RECIPES 19

Ham And Cheese Dijon Sandwich 20

Spinach Oregano Green Pepper Beef Pie 21

Beacon Ham Combo Muffins 22

Glazed Coated Pumpkin Donuts 23

Perfect Beef Onion Burgers 25

Beef Green Chilies Burritos 27

Ground Beef Beans Casserole 28

Roasted Figs And Sausages Maple Glazed 29

Fish and Potato Chips 30

BREAD RECIPES 32

Mushroom Onion Stuffed Bread 33

Simple Pizza Crust 34

Raisins Walnut Honey Bread 35

Oats Sauerkraut Bacon Sausage Roll 36

Ricotta Cherry Bread Toast 38

Graham Jolly Bread 39

Flavored Banana Lemon Bread 40

Flatbread With Sausage Marinara Sauce Toppings .. 41

Cinnamon Strawberry Bread 42

VEGETABLES RECIPES 44

Tomatoes Shallots Convection Roast........................45

Black Bean Cheesy Flautas..46

Buddha Bowl...47

Benny's Potatoes Jive 49

Roasted Veggies With Lemon And Olives 50

My Special Veggies Turkey Meat Pie 51

Crispy Roasted Broccoli With Garlic..........................52

Root Vegetable Roast 53

Coated Rosemary Mixture Vegetables Toast............54

BEEF PORKS AND LAMB RECIPES 55

BBQ Sauce Cheesy Meatloaf......................................56

Italian Mustard Pork Chops 57

Honey Ketchup Meat Loaf 58

Onion, Sage Meatloaf 59

Skewed Meatball Kebobs..60

Vegetable Beef Slow Roast 61

Roast Pork Tenderloin..63

Ground Beef Tomatoes Jalo Nachos 64

Apple Onion Pork Loin 65

Soft Horseradish Rib Roast 66

SEAFOOD RECIPES..67

Perfect Cooked Salmon Fillet.....................................68

Soy Miso Sake-Glazed Salmon 69

Convection Broiled Lobster Tails 70

Coconut Crackers Crispy Tilapia 70

Gouda Magic Shrimp Scampi 72

Convection Oven Prawns 74

Halibut In Mushroom Sherry Sauce 75

Easy Flakes Halibut With Scallop And Shrimp Prep time: 10 minutes 76

White Cod Fillet Gondola 77

Orange Fennel Fish Fillet 78

POULTRY AND CHICKEN RECIPES 79

Convection Chicken Wings 80

Tomatoes Baby Spinach Chicken Casseroles 80

Turkey Oats Meatloaf 81

Chicken_Bebita 83

Spaghetti Chicken Casserole 84

Chang Chicken Casserole 85

Roasted Chicken Breast With Prosciutto Green Beans 86

Cheez-it Tender Chicken 87

Cream Cheese Worcestershire Chicken Breast 89

Tasty Buffalo Wings 90

Chicken Mini Chimichangas 91

Walnut Honey Chicken Breast 92

Roasted Duck With White Vermouth And shallot 93

Tender Cooked Duck With Currant Jelly Glazed 94

Chicken Ham Schnitzel Cordon Bleu 95

APPERTIZERS AND SNACKS RECIPES 96

French Toast Pumpkin Walnuts Casserole................97

Browned Oven Crispy Granola..................................98

Jumbo Jet Shells...99

Brie Cheese Apricot Puffed Pastry 100

Cinnamon Smokies Wraps 101

Cheesy Ginger Chili Bread 102

Bacon Chicken Thighs 103

Merry Bells Pizzas 104

Convection Baked Gnocchi Alfredo 105

Spaghetti Beef Lasagna Rolls 106

DESSERT RECIPES 107

Peach Lemon Pies 108

Amazing Peanut Butter Cookies 109

Churros With Chocolate Cream Sauce 110

Best Dessert Cake 112

Stylist Monkey Bread 113

Vanilla Peanut Butter Cookies 114

Convection Toaster Brownies 116

Oatmeal Raisin Cookies 118

INTRODUCTION

Understanding The Convection Oven

What is Convection Oven

In case you are wondering what the heck is an air convection oven, the quick answer is a convection oven, an oven that comes along with a fan and exhaust system.

A convection oven has a similar structure to a standard oven: It has a rectangular shape with a transparent front door that allows you to see food that is being cooked inside. What makes it different from the traditional oven is the convection setting.

What is Convection Setting?

The convection setting introduces a convection mechanism (a fan attached to the interior) to circulate hot air that is to be blown around and onto food at high speed; literally, it produces extra energy that meets the surface of the roast forcefully, which crisps up the outer surface of the food.

The convection oven kitchen appliance is used for cooking almost anything. It can be used to cook meat, veggies, or fries. You can bake, grill, or broil with it.

Does Convection Oven Cook Faster Than A Conventional Oven?

A convection oven cooks 25 to 30 % faster than regular ovens at 25% lower temperature. Convection ovens are hotter because of the extra force/energy they produce. Depending on the fan's power, they produce about 25 to 30% extra energy. The convection oven is hotter and faster than the conventional oven.

The convection oven operates by circulating hot air around food through an exhaust system and a fan. Meaning, food is endlessly engulfed in a cozy environment, so there is no need moving food around while cooking. Yet, it still achieves a beautiful outcome of a nice golden-brown color. It's either you cook at a lower temperature of 25 to 30 percent or the same temperature at a reduced cooking time, but always keep an eye on the food from time to time.

Tips For Cooking With The Convection Oven

The convection oven produces extra energy in the form of hot air that is distributed through the fan located inside the oven. The whooshing air comes in contact with the surface of the food, so the surface cooks faster than the inside of the food. Although the hot air does not come in contact with the interior of the food but the hotness of the oven will be cooking food simultaneously from the outer side.

Convection ovens are perfect in a situation where you want to roast large meat cuts but you want the outside to be nicely brown and medium rare on the inside. This includes all beef in general, apart from pork, that needs to be cooked medium.

In general, roasting meats in a convection oven can dry out the meat's surface, and the force of the hot air having direct contact with the surface of the roast can shrink the food, unlike in conventional ovens. It's advised mostly to make a few adjustments when you are roasting meats.

Although, when cooking with the convection ovens, you have a choice of either reducing the temperature or shortening cooking time or a bit of both. But when cooking chicken and turkey, they have to be cooked properly, as in cooked into the deepest side all the way. And since the hot air isn't blowing into the interior of the meat, it's best to reduce the cooking temperature and leave the cooking time as it is.

Additional Convection Tips

The hot air that the oven produces blows from the back and rotates all over the oven, this is because in most convection ovens you find the fan located at the back. You may want to use pans that are not high to allow the radiant heat have a better effect on the food. Most of the time, it's best to keep food uncovered when cooking in the convection oven, unless the recipe instructions say otherwise.

Quick bread, cakes, and most baked foods that begin as liquid batter do not do quite well in these kinds of ovens. The force of the whooshing air can leave an effect on the batter that will come out as it is in the finished product.

How To Use Different Settings On Convection Oven

The Main Differences
A conventional oven is comprised of at least two heating elements located at the bottom and top. Baking and roasting require the same heat element. A convection oven uses a convection mechanism to circulate air. Baking and roasting are also done by circulating hot air around the food at a high speed.

Baking:
Baking requires a longer time compared to roasting food, it involves cooking the inside of food evenly while browning the outside with constant medium heat.
It is preferable to bake meatloaf, fish, and skinless poultry instead of roasting because the surface of food can easily burn or dry out because of the high heat involved in roasting. Bread, pies, and cakes, are mostly baked.

Roasting:

Roasting requires a shorter time; it starts off with high heat to brown food quickly for the crisp outer skin, then finishes off with lower heat until the food is properly cooked through. Roast prime rib, skin-on, or whole poultry and dense vegetables like carrots and potatoes.

Broiling:

Broiling gives almost the same effect as when you grill, it uses only the top heat element, so food is cooked and browned quickly. Broil tender cuts of meat, such as pork chops or steaks. The broiling setting is also used to finish food earlier prepared in the oven or stovetop—melt cheese on top of baked poultry, etc. It only takes a few minutes to broil food, so you have to be on the lookout. Place the food you want to broil on the top oven rack, about 3 or 4 inches away from the heat source.

Convection baking uses the convection mechanism to produce heat, and the fan helps to circulate the hot air around. The radiant heat will not have any direct contact with food.

Convection roast works using the fan, along with the heating elements on the top. What it does is control heat by rotating over baking and broiling elements as needed.

What Can You Cook In The Convection Oven?

A typical air convection oven is a multi-functional kitchen appliance that will most likely be able to, bake, toast, air fry, broil, and keep food warm.
You cannot just cook everything in the convection oven because of the fan. Most delicate foods that starts as liquid batter do not do quite well in the convection oven, such as, custards, quick breads and soufflés. The force of the whooshing air can leave an effect in the batter that will come out as it is in the finished product.

How To Convert Traditional Oven Recipes For Convection Oven

Basically, so many traditional oven recipes I have come across on the net generally specify the cooking time and temperature. So I guess you should not have a problem converting your old traditional oven recipes to suit your air fryer oven recipes.

The thumb rule It either you cook at a lower temperature or reduce the cooking time, or simply do both. The simplest method is to reduce the cooking temperature by 25 percent than what the recipe calls for. Let's say a recipe calls for 400 degrees F. You can reduce it to 375 F.

But note this! Some convection ovens are built to automatically adjust by themselves. Meaning, the oven can adjust your setting from 400 to 375 to compensate for the extra hotness. So study your model manual well to understand how your oven operates and how to make adjustments.

Alternatively, you can also reduce the cooking time by 25% and leave the temperature the same. (Based on the assumption that your oven does not self-adjust itself). But note, it is advised to shorten the cooking temperature by 30 degrees when roasting meats and 25 degrees for pies and cookies.

In conclusion, a broadly accurate guide or principle for cooking in the convection oven is to check your food a bit early because the convection oven generally cooks the food quicker than a conventional oven.

Study your product's cooking instructions and observe the complete cooking cycle for foods. This will help you get used to your appliance. Keep a close eye on the food every 12–15 minutes and observe the smell. The smell can give you a hint about the cooking. Once it starts to smell, check every now and then until it's cooked to your satisfaction.

BREAKFAST RECIPES

Ham-Cheese Scallions Omelet Frittatas

Prep time: 20 minutes
Cook time: 43 minutes
Servings: 24

INGREDIENTS

1/8 tsp of black pepper
1/8 tsp of dried thyme
2 tbsp of scallions, minced
1/3 cup of low fat extra sharp cheddar cheese
4 large egg whites
1 large egg
2/3 cup of low sodium ham, finely chopped
1/2 cup of onion, finely chopped
1 tsp of olive oil

INSTRUCTIONS

1. Heat up the oven to 350 F.
2. Heat the oil over medium heat in a non-stick fry pan. Add onion and ham and sauté until the onion is soft and translucent; set aside to cool.
3. Whisk the eggs, egg whites, scallions, black pepper, thyme, cheese, cooled onion, and ham together in a large bowl.
4. Spray the 24 mini muffin tins thoroughly with non-stick spray. Fill muffin tins with the egg mixture.
5. Place in the oven and bake for 17-20 minutes or until set.

Cinnamon French Toast

Prep time: 20 minutes

Cook time: 16 minutes

Servings: 4 slices

INGREDIENTS

2 tsp of cinnamon (optional)

4 tsp of sugar

1/2- 1 cup of milk (I used almond milk)

4 eggs

4 slices of bread

INSTRUCTIONS

1. In a shallow dish, whisk together the milk, eggs, and sugar until smooth.
2. Dip each of the bread slices in the egg mixture and allow each side to soak for at least 5 minutes.
3. Line your baking sheet with foil and arrange the soaked bread slices over the baking sheet.
4. Heat the oven to 350 F. Place the pan in the oven and cook for 7 minutes on each side.
5. To make it crispier, set to"Toast" mode on your toaster oven, to level 4, and toast both sides.

6. Serve with berry sauce and butter with maple syrup.

Falafel Tzatziki Sauce Tacos

Prep time: minutes
Cook time: 10 minutes
Servings:
INGREDIENTS
1 package of Corn and Wheat tortillas
1 container of Tzatziki sauce
1 package of Trader Joe's Falafel
Optional garnish: thinly sliced red onion
Finely chopped jalepeno pepper for garnish (Optional)
INSTRUCTIONS
1. Heat up the oven to 350 F, place the frozen falafel the air fryer oven, and heat for 10 minutes.
2. Allow the falafel to cool down until you can handle, cut in half.
3. Stacks about four tortillas in the Microwave and heat for 30 seconds.
4. Spread the sauce generously over the tortilla, layer each tortilla with three pieces of falafel over the sauce, and garnish with onions and peppers.

Baby Spinach Scallions Casserole Frittata

Prep time: 10 minutes
Cook time: 20 minutes
Servings: 4

INGREDIENTS

8 oz of crumbled Feta
4 scallions thinly sliced (white and green parts)
1-pint grape tomatoes, halved
1 5-oz bag of baby spinach
1/2 tsp of black pepper
2 tsp of kosher salt
10 large eggs
3 tbsp of olive oil

INSTRUCTIONS

1. Preheat the oven to 350°F.
2. In a 2-quart casserole, add olive oil and heat in the oven for 5 minutes.
3. Whisk the eggs, pepper and salt together in a bowl. Add the scallions, tomatoes, and spinach. Fold in the Feta.
4. Withdraw the casserole dish from the oven, and pour in the egg mixture. Bake for 25 to 30 minutes until the frittata is slightly puffed and the edges are browned and a knife inserted comes out clean.

Convection Crumbled Bacon With Sweet Potatoes

Prep time: 5 minutes
Cook time: 60 minutes
Servings: 2

INGREDIENTS

(Optional) pure maple syrup for drizzling
4 cooked eggs, to your liking
3 center-cut slices of bacon (cooked and crumbled)
Coarse sea salt
1 tbsp of olive oil
2 small sweet potatoes

INSTRUCTIONS

1. Heat up the oven to 400 F. Make multiple holes in the sweet potatoes with a fork.
2. Lightly coat each potato with half a tablespoon of olive oil and a pinch of sea salt.
3. Roast the potatoes for about 45-60 minutes, or until fork tender.
4. Now you can cook up eggs to your liking. Cut the sweet potatoes deep from the center using a knife, leaving about an inch uncut.
5. Place 2 cooked eggs in the middle of each potato and generously sprinkle with crumbled bacon. Drizzle top with maple syrup and serve.

Oatmeal Bars With Blueberries Pumpkin

Prep time: 5 minutes
Cook time: 30 minutes
Servings: 9

INGREDIENTS

Base:

1 scoop Vanilla Whey Protein
1 1/2 tsp of vanilla
2 bananas
1 1/2 tsp of cinnamon
1 tsp of kosher salt
1 tbsp of coconut oil
4 tablespoons honey
1 cup of slivered almonds
2 cups of old fashioned oats

Topping:

1/4 tsp of cinnamon
1/4 cup of coconut-almond milk, plain almond milk or plain coconut milk
1 cup of fresh organic blueberries
1/4 cup of pumpkin seeds
1/4 cup of slivered almonds
1/2 cup of old fashioned oats
9 x 9 baking pan

INSTRUCTIONS

Base:

1. Heat the oven to 350 F.
2. Line your pan using parchment paper, and grease lightly with coconut oil.
3. Add oats, Whey Protein, bananas, slivered almonds, vanilla, coconut oil, honey, and salt to a food processor and process for several minutes until completely combined and wet.

4. Pour the mixture into the baking pan, and spread it out evenly. Smooth the top with an offset spatula. Place in the oven and bake for 8–10 minutes.

Topping:

5. In a medium bowl, combine the ingredients until combined.

6. Remove pan from the oven, spread the mixture over base and lightly press down. Return to the oven for another 15 minutes of baking.

Veggie Omelet

Prep time: 20 minutes
Cook time: 35 minutes
Servings: 5-6

INGREDIENTS

2 pinch black pepper
2 cup of milk
10-12 eggs
2 cup of chopped breakfast sausage
1/2 cup of chopped red peppers
1/2 cup of chopped green peppers
1/2 tsp of powdered garlic

INSTRUCTIONS

1. Preheat the oven to 375°F and grease a large baking pan lightly.
1. Beat the milk and eggs together in a large mixing bowl. Beat in the remaining ingredients until nicely combined.
2. Place the mixture to the greased pan and cover top with foil.
3. Bake for 35 minutes until set.

Sausage Cheese Casserole

Prep Time: 15 minutes
Cook Time: 30 minutes
Servings: 12

INGREDIENTS

8 eggs, beaten
2 cups of shredded mozzarella cheese
1 teaspoon of dried oregano
2 cups of shredded Cheddar cheese
1 pound of pork sausage
1 (8 oz) package of refrigerated crescent roll dough

INSTRUCTIONS

1. Cook the sausages in a large cooking pot over medium-high heat until all the sausages are brown. Drain, mash and set aside.
2. Preheat the oven to 300 degrees F. Add a little grease to a 9x13-inch casserole dish.
3. Spread the crescent roll dough at the bottom of the prepared casserole dish, coat with the crumbled sausage.
4. Mix mozzarella, cheddar, and beaten eggs in a large bowl. Add oregano to season the mixture. Pour the egg mixture over the sausage and crescent rolls.

5. Place in the oven and bake until a skewer inserted in the center comes out clean, about 25 to 30 minutes

Convection Oven Omelet

Prep time: 10 minutes
Cook time: 35 minutes
Servings: 2
INGREDIENTS
110 grams of extra-sharp Cheddar, diced
Extra grated cheese, for garnish
40 grams of spring onion, chopped the green and white parts
1/2 tsp of freshly ground black pepper
1 tsp of salt
2 tbsp of milk or cream
5 extra-large eggs
1 tbsp of minced jalapeno pepper
75 grams of chopped yellow onion
180 grams of Yukon gold potato, medium-diced
1 tbsp of unsalted butter
110 grams of good thick-cut bacon (cut into 2 cm slices crosswise)

INSTRUCTIONS

1. Heat up the oven to 350 F.
2. Brown the bacon slices in a stainless steel nonstick frying pan (20 cm) over medium-low heat for 5 to 7 minutes, stirring frequently.
3. Transfer cooked bacon on paper towels and let drain, discard cooking fat.

4. Melt butter over medium-low heat and cook the yellow onion and potato for about 10 minutes, tossing periodically, until onion begins to brown and the potato is soft yet firm. Add in the jalapeno pepper and continue cooking for an extra 30 seconds.
5. While the potato is cooking, beat together the milk, eggs, pepper, and salt with a fork in a medium bowl. Stir in the diced Cheddar and spring onions.
6. Add cooked bacon to potato in the pan and pour the egg mixture on top.
7. Bake in the oven at 350 F for 15 to 20 minutes,(you can start checking after 12 minutes) or until omelet puff up and centre is almost cooked.
8. Sprinkle top with extra cheese and bake for 1 minute more. Serve immediately directly from the pan.

Early Morning Hash

Prep time: 10 minutes

Cook time: 20 minutes

Servings: 4-6

INGREDIENTS

1 tsp of paprika

1/2 stick of unsalted butter, melted

1/2 cup of mixed frozen vegetables (green beans, carrots, corn)

1 small yellow onion, chopped in Half-inch pieces

3/4 cup of precooked kielbasa, cut in Half-inch pieces

1 3/4 cups of peeled russet potatoes, cut in Half-inch pieces

1 tsp of kosher salt

INSTRUCTIONS

1. Preheat the oven to 400 F degrees.
2. Add the frozen vegetables, kielbasa, potatoes, and chopped onion in a large bowl. Toss with paprika, melted butter, and salt to coat.
3. Evenly distribute the coated ingredients in the baking pan.
4. Place the pan in the oven and bake for 20 minutes. Remove the pan from the oven, and stir well with a spatula or wooden spoon. Place the pan back in the oven and bake for an additional 10 minutes. Remove and let sit for 5 minutes, slice, and serve.

LUNCH RECIPES

Ham And Cheese Dijon Sandwich

Prep Time: 15 minutes
Cook Time: 20 minutes
Servings: 24

INGREDIENTS

1 1/2 teaspoons of Worcestershire sauce
1 pound of Swiss cheese, thinly sliced
1 pound of cooked deli ham, thinly sliced
1 1/2 tablespoons of poppy seeds
1 tablespoon of dried minced onion
24 mini sandwich rolls
3/4 cup of melted butter
1 1/2 tablespoons of Dijon mustard

INSTRUCTIONS

1. Preheat the oven to 325 degrees F.
2. Lightly grease a 9x13-inch baking dish with cooking spray. Mix dijon mustard, poppy seeds, Worcestershire sauce, dried onion, and butter together in a bowl.
3. Separate the roll tops from the bottoms, then arrange the bottom pieces in the earlier prepared baking dish.
4. Spread about half the ham on the rolls. Spread the cheese on the ham, and layer the remaining ham slices on top.
5. Place the separated top rolls on the sandwiches. Evenly spread the mustard mixture over the rolls.
6. Place rolls in the preheated oven and bake until the cheese is melted and the rolls are a bit browned, about 20 minutes. Slice the rolls to serve.

Spinach Oregano Green Pepper Beef Pie

Prep time: 25 minutes

Cook time: 30 minutes plus standing

Servings: 8

INGREDIENTS

1 large tomato, seeded and diced

2 cups of shredded cheddar cheese, divided

3 large eggs, lightly beaten

1 (10 ounces) package of frozen chopped spinach, thawed and squeezed dry

1/4 tsp of pepper

1/2 tsp of dried marjoram

1/2 tsp of dried basil

1 tsp of dried oregano

1 tsp of salt

1/4 cup of ketchup

1 minced clove garlic

1 medium chopped green pepper

1 medium chopped onion

1 lb of ground beef

2-3 tbsp of cold water

7 tbsp of cold butter

1/3 cup of old-fashioned oats

1 cup of all-purpose flour

INSTRUCTIONS

1. Combine together the oats and flour in a large bowl; add in the butter and cut in with a knife until crumbly.

2. Slowly pour in tbsp of cold water, tossing with a fork until it forms a dough ball.

3. Roll the dough out to 9-inches wide, place it in the pie plate, trim, and use two hands to flute the edges.

4. Cook the onion, beef, green pepper, and garlic in a large skillet over medium heat until the meat is no longer pink; drain.

5. Stir in the seasonings and ketchup. Gently mix in the spinach and let it cool slightly.
6. Stir in 1 cup cheese and eggs until nicely combined; spoon mixture into crust.
7. Bake in the oven for 25-30 minutes at 375 F, or until the center is set.
8. Remove pan and sprinkle pie around edges with tomato and the rest cheese.
9. Return to the oven and bake for additional 5-10 minutes or until the cheese is melted. Let it cool for about 10 minutes before slicing. Serve alongside fresh fruit or salad.

Beacon Ham Combo Muffins

Prep time: 15 minutes
Cook time: 20 minutes
Servings: 12
INGREDIENTS
1/2 cup of shredded cheese
1/2 cup of diced bacon
1/2 cup of diced ham
2 small eggs (beaten)
2/6 cup of milk
1 1/8 cup of bisquick mix
INSTRUCTIONS
1. Preheat the oven to 450 F degrees. Spray two muffin pans with cooking spray.
2. Prepare Bisquick Drop biscuits according to package directions.
3. Spoon about 1 tablespoon of biscuit mix into each muffin tin.
4. In a bowl, beat the beaten egg, diced bacon, half of the cheese, and diced ham.

5. Spoon the egg/bacon mix over each biscuit mix. Distribute a bit of the remaining cheese on top each.
6. Bake in the preheated oven for 10 to 13 minutes or until the cheese start to brown on top.

Glazed Coated Pumpkin Donuts

Prep time: 10 minutes
Cook time: 9 minutes
Servings: 12
INGREDIENTS
1/2 tsp of pumpkin pie spice
1/4 tsp of fine grain sea salt
1/8 tsp of baking soda
1/4 tsp of baking powder
1/2 cup of white whole wheat flour
1/4 cup of coconut sugar, (or brown sugar)
1/4 tsp of real vanilla extract
1/4 cup of pureed pumpkin plus 1 tablespoon
2 tbsp of melted coconut oil plus extra for greasing
1 large egg
CINNAMON MAPLE GLAZE:
2 tbsp of unsweetened plain almond milk
1/8 tsp of ground cinnamon
2 tsp of real maple syrup
1 tbsp of coconut butter
INSTRUCTIONS
1. Heat the oven to 400 F and grease mini donut pan.
2. Mix the pumpkin pureed, egg, vanilla and coconut oil together in a medium bowl until well combined. Add coconut sugar and stir.
3. Sprinkle top of the mixture with flour, baking soda, baking powder, pumpkin pie spice and salt and stir just until combined.
4. Spoon batter into a greased mini donut pan.

5. Place the donut pan in the oven, and bake for about 8 to 9 minutes or until the donut is set.
Let cool for 5 minutes in the pan, then place onto a wire rack to completely cool.
For the Glaze:
6. Combine together the cinnamon, maple syrup and coconut butter. Slowly stir in almond milk until the desired consistency is reached. Coat the cooled donuts in glaze.
Notes
The glaze will darken in color and takes appx 30 minutes to set.

Perfect Beef Onion Burgers

Prep time: 15 minutes
Cook time: 15 minutes
Servings: 4-6

INGREDIENTS

2 tbsp of ketchup
1 large egg, slightly beaten
1/2 cup of crushed saltine crackers
1 1/2 tsp of worcestershire sauce
Half envelop of dry onion soup mix
1 pound of ground beef
Salt and pepper, to taste

INSTRUCTIONS

1. Heat the oven to 450 degrees. Spray your baking pan with non-stick spray.
2. Mix all ingredients in a medium bowl without over-mixing.
3. Mold the mixture evenly into about 4 to 6 portions, then transfer to greased baking pan.
4. Bake in the oven for about 12–15 minutes; flipping the burgers halfway through the cooking, until the burgers are cooked through. Cooking time depends on the size of the patty.

Veggies Pizza Sauce Bagels

Prep time: 10 minutes
Cook time: 15 minutes
Servings: 1

INGREDIENTS

Mushroom pieces, black olives, onions or favorite veggies preference
Pepperoni, sausage or favorite meat
1/2 cup of mozzarella cheese or Parmesan cheese
4 tbsp of pizza sauce
1 bagel cut in halves

INSTRUCTIONS

1. Heat the oven to 450 F.
2. Spoon two tbsp. pizza sauce over each half bagel.
3. Sprinkle tops of each bagel half with 1/4 cup of mozzarella

cheese. Top with preference pizza toppings
4. Transfer the bagel to the oven and bake for 10 minutes, or until the bagel is slightly browned and the cheese has melted.

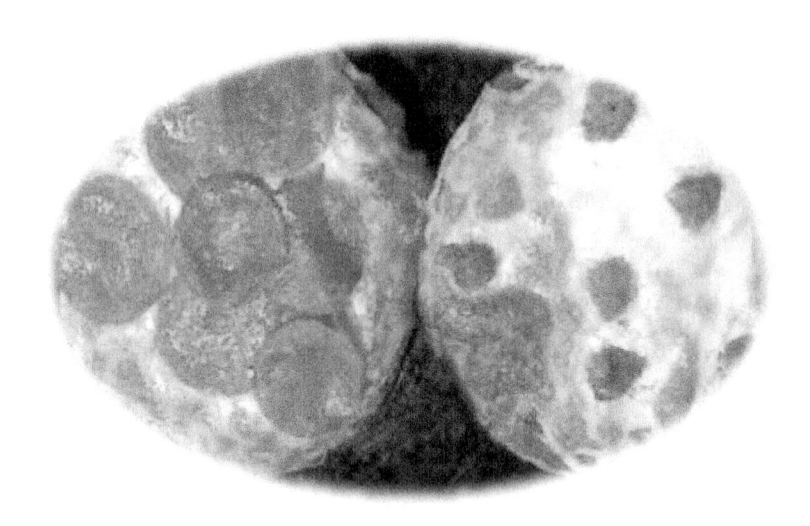

Beef Green Chilies Burritos

Prep time: 10 minutes
Cook time: 1 hour 25 minutes
Servings: 4

INGREDIENTS

18 flour tortillas (can use less of a larger tortilla) 6 inches or less
1 cup of low-fat Colby jack cheese, divided
1 (4-ounce) can of black olives, sliced
1 (4-ounce) can of green chilies, diced
1 (16-ounce) can of refried beans, fat-free
1 tbsp of cumin
2 tbsp of chili powder
4 chopped clove garlic
1 (28-ounce) can of diced tomatoes (reserve the juice)
1 1/2 pounds of lean ground beef

GARNISHES

Salsa
Guacamole
Sour cream
Shredded lettuce

INSTRUCTIONS

1. Heat oven to 375 F.
2. Brown the ground beef over medium-high heat in a large skillet, drain beef and rinse.
3. Place meat back into the skillet, and reduce to medium heat. Add refried beans, can of diced tomatoes, half cup of reserved juice, green chilies, chili powder, black olives, cumin, half a cup of cheese, and garlic. Cook for about 10 minutes, or until everything is well combined.
4. Spoon about 1/3 cup of the mix into each tortilla, then roll up, and place seam side facing down in a greased baking dish.
5. Pour any remaining beef mix around the tortillas. Sprinkle with the remaining cheese.
6. Bake in the oven until cheese bubbles, about 20 minutes. Garnish with salsa, guacamole, sour cream, and shredded lettuce.

Ground Beef Beans Casserole

Prep time: 15 minutes
Cook time: 60 minutes
Servings: 4

INGREDIENTS

1/2 cup of water
1 can of cream of chicken soup
1 pkg of taco seasoning
2 cup of shredded cheddar cheese, divided
1 small chopped onion
1 can of ro-tel tomatoes
1 (10-12 ounce) bag of tortilla chips, crushed
1 can of ranch style beans
1 pounds of ground beef

INSTRUCTIONS

1. Heat up the oven to 325 F. Grease a 9×13 casserole dish.
2. Brown the meat in a large skillet over medium-high heat until brown, and drain off fat.
3. Stir in the tomatoes, beans, soup, onion, taco seasoning, and water. Simmer until well blended and heated over medium-low heat.
4. Spoon meat/bean mixture over a layer of crushed tortilla chips. Repeat layers.
5. Place in the greased casserole dish and cover with foil. Bake in the oven until bubbly, about 20 to 30 minutes. Remove from the oven and let sit for about 10 minutes before serving. Garnish with sour cream and salsa.

Roasted Figs And Sausages Maple Glazed

Prep time: 30 minutes
Cook time: 10 minutes
Servings: 4

INGREDIENTS

2 tsp of olive oil
1 1/2 pounds of Swiss chard
1/2 large sweet onion
8 ripe fresh figs
2 package of fully cooked chicken with roasted garlic sausages
2 tbsp of balsamic vinegar
2 tbsp of maple syrup
Salt and pepper

INSTRUCTIONS

1. Heat up the oven to 450 F. Line your oven tray with foil.
2. Stir one tablespoon of vinegar with the syrup in a small bowl until well blended.
3. In a single layer, place sausages and figs on the prepared oven tray, and brush top lightly with 1 tbsp of syrup mixture.
4. Roast sausages and figs in the oven for 8 to 10 minutes, flipping and brushing with the remaining 1 tbsp of syrup mixture midway through roasting.

5. While the sausage and fig are roasting, add onion to a heat-proof bowl. Cover bowl with plastic wrap with holes, and microwave for 3 minutes on High.
6. Remove bowl from oven, add chard to bowl; cover and continue to microwave for 9 minutes, stirring once or until vegetables are soft.
7. Stir in the remaining 1 tablespoon vinegar, oil, 1/4 of ground black pepper, and 1/4 teaspoon of salt. Serve chard with sausages and figs.
(If your oven is small, you may need to cook the sausages and figs in two batches.)

Fish and Potato Chips
Prep time: 10 minutes
Cook time: 42 minutes
Servings: 4
INGREDIENTS
2 tbsp of capers, drained
1 thinly sliced clove garlic
1 lemon, halved, thinly slice on half
4 6-oz of cod pieces
8 sprigs fresh thyme
1 1/4 tsp of black pepper
1 1/4 tsp of kosher salt
4 tbsp of olive oil
1 3/4 lbs of red potatoes, cut into 1-inch chunks
INSTRUCTIONS
1. Preheat the oven to 450°F.
2. Place 2 tablespoons of the oil, potatoes, 4 sprigs of the thyme, 1/4 teaspoon of the pepper and 1 teaspoon of the salt in the -oven tray and toss.
3. Spread the mixture in the tray in a single layer. Place tray in the oven and bake for 25 to 30 minutes, stirring occasionally, until golden.
4. Cut a large piece of aluminum foil, transfer the roasted potatoes, and wrap to keep warm. Clean the tray for another use. Place cod pieces in tray.

5. Add half lemon slices, capers, garlic remaining thyme sprigs, pepper and salt on top the cod. Drizzle top with the remaining oil.
6. Bake in the oven for 8 to 12 minutes, or until cooked through.
7. Divide potatoes and cod amongst individual plates. Top with a squeeze of the remaining half lemon and return to oven until the juices are warmed through, about 5 minutes. Pour the sauce over the fish and potatoes.

BREAD RECIPES

Mushroom Onion Stuffed Bread

Prep time: 2 hr 15 minutes
Cook time: 50 minutes
Servings: 3-4 loaves

INGREDIENTS

1/4 tsp of pepper
1 cup of wheat germ
2 cups of milk
2 pkg of active dry yeast (1/4 ounce)
1 egg
1/2 cup of warm water (115 degrees)
8 all-purpose of un-sifted all purpose flour
1/4 cup of butter
4 tsp of salt
3 Tbsp of molasses
1 cup of finely chopped onion
1/2 pound of mushrooms, finely chopped

INSTRUCTIONS

1. Heat the butter in a saucepan over low heat. Sauté the onion and mushrooms in pan until the liquid has evaporated and the onion is tender. Set aside to cool.
2. Bring milk to a boil in a clean and dry small saucepan, reduce heat and let is simmer for 2 minutes (Scalding).
3. Stir in the molasses, pepper and salt. Allow cooling to lukewarm.
4. Mix together half a cup of warm water with the yeast in a large warm bowl stir until dissolved.
5. Combine the mushroom mixture, milk mixture, egg and wheat germ. Gradually add in 2 cups of flour until no lumps form. Stir in more flour until a stiff dough is formed. Knead the dough until smooth.
6. Set aside in a warm place until doubled in size.
7. Divide into 3 to 4-portions. Set aside to rise again to almost double in size.
8. Bake at 350 degrees for 50 minutes in the oven, or until it gives a hollow sound when tapped on top. Allow to cool before serving.

Simple Pizza Crust

Prep time: 15 minutes
Cook time: 15 minutes
Servings: 2 crust

INGREDIENTS

2 tablespoons of olive oil
1/2 teaspoon of salt
1 pkg of active dry yeast
1/2 cup of water (115 degrees) or half flat beer and half water
3 1/2 to 4 cups of flour

INSTRUCTIONS

1. In a large warm bowl, dissolve the yeast in 1/4 cup of warm water.
2. Combine olive oil, 2 cups flour, remaining water, and salt in a large bowl until no lump forms and a soft dough is formed. (For extra flavor, you can use 3/4 cup of flat beer plus 3/4 cup of water). Stir in the yeast mixture.
4. Stir in more flour until a stiff dough is formed.
5. Turn dough out on a floured surface, and knead until the dough is smooth.
6. Transfer dough to a greased bowl, and turn repeatedly to grease dough top. Set aside for a few minutes, until doubled in size.
7. Punch the dough down and divide it into two. Mold the dough with slightly oily hands into two 12-inch balls, then roll them out to form 2 pizzas. Add your desired toppings.
8. Bake in the oven at 325 degrees for 15 minutes until bubbly.

Raisins Walnut Honey Bread

Prep time: 15 minutes
Cook time: 75 minutes
Servings: 4 loaves
INGREDIENTS
1/2 cup of chopped walnuts
1/2 cup of raisins
4 cup of all purpose flour
1 cup of honey
1 tsp of baking soda
1/2 cup of vegetable oil
1/2 cup of milk
4 eggs
1/2 tsp of ground allspice
1/2 tsp of ground cloves
1 tsp of ground cinnamon
1 cup of sugar
INSTRUCTIONS
1. Mix together the eggs, cinnamon, allspice, cloves and sugar in a large bowl. Stir in vegetable oil and milk and mix in the

baking soda.
2. Bring honey to a boil in a small pot, and stir the honey into the flour mixture.
3. Fold in walnuts and raisins, stir for 10 minutes with a strong spoon by hand. Let sit for 60 minutes.
4. Heat up the oven to 325 F. Grease Four 8 by 4-inch loaf pans. Pour the batter into each loaf pan, filling about 2 inches.
5. Bake in the oven for about 1 hour and 15 minutes until a knife inserted in the center comes out clean and the bread is lightly brown. Bread will have cracks on top.

Oats Sauerkraut Bacon Sausage Roll
Prep time: 20 minutes
Cook time: 1 hr 30 minutes
Servings: 4-6
INGREDIENTS
1/2 tsp of Worcestershire sauce
4 slice of bacon
3 tbsp of chopped onion
2 tsp of caraway seeds
16 ounces of sauerkraut snipped
1/4 cup of shredded Swiss cheese
1 pound of pork sausage
1 slightly beaten egg
1/2 cup of oats, quick cooking
12 by 8-inch baking dish
1 tsp of salt
INSTRUCTIONS
1. Combine Worcestershire sauce, oats, sausage, and salt; blend well. Make a 10 by 7 rectangle using waxed paper.
2. Combine the caraway seeds, sauerkraut, and onion in a mixing bowl. Spread the sauerkraut mix on the sausage rectangle evenly. Roll it up jelly-roll style.
3. Arrange slices of bacon on top. Place rolls in the baking dish.
4. Bake in the oven for 80-90 minutes at 350 degrees. Cover it

with foil for the first hour of baking time. It helps io reduce crusty surface,
5. Once it is 5 minutes to the last cooking time, remove from the oven and sprinkle the top with cheese, then place back to melt cheese.

Ricotta Cherry Bread Toast

Prep time: 20 minutes
Cook time: 35 minutes
Servings: 8

INGREDIENTS

2 tablespoons of lemon juice
Flaky sea salt
1/2 cup of slivered almonds, toasted
8 (½ inch thick) whole-grain artisan bread, toasted
Pinch of salt to taste
2 cups of part-skim ricotta cheese
4 teaspoons of extra-virgin olive oil
4 cups of pitted fresh cherries
2 teaspoons of lemon zest
2 tablespoons of honey, plus more for serving
2 teaspoons of fresh thyme

INSTRUCTIONS

1. Heat up your oven to 350 degrees F.
2. Toss cherries with oil, salt, lemon juice, and honey.
3. Place the mixture on a parchment-lined, rimmed baking sheet and roast for 12-15 minutes, shaking once or twice during cooking, until the cherries are soft and warm.
4. Top the toasted bread with almonds, cherries, lemon zest, ricotta cheese, sea salt and thyme. If desired, drizzle with more honey.

Graham Jolly Bread

Prep time: 35 minutes
Cook time: 50 minutes
Servings: 2 loaves

INGREDIENTS

2 cup of graham flour
1 Tbsp of salt
1/3 cup of molasses or dark corn syrup
3 Tbsp of vegetable oil
6 1/2 to 7 cups of all purpose white flour
3 cups of warm water
1 pkg of active dry yeast

INSTRUCTIONS

1. Combine 1 cup warm water with yeast in a large bowl until dissolved, let stand for 5 minutes. Add in 1-1/2 cups of the flour and whisk until smooth.
2. Place dough in a warm place, and cover loosely with a light towel for 45 minutes or until it has risen.
3. Pour the remaining two cups of warm water, vegetable oil, molasses, graham flour, and salt in a bowl. Beat with an electric mixer at medium speed until smooth.
4. Gradually stir in extra white flour by hand little by little and mixing well as you add until soft dough is formed.
5. Lightly sprinkle flour on a work surface, turn dough out and knead for about 7 to 10 minutes, or until dough is smooth and elastic. Transfer to a greased bowl, turn once to grease.
6. Place in a warm place, cover with a for towel and let rise about 1-1/2 hours or until doubled in size.
7. Divide the dough into 2 equal portions and shape into loaves. Transfer dough into two greased loaf pans. Cover for about 1 hour or until increased in size.
8. Place pans in the oven and bake for 50 minutes at 375 degrees or until they're done. Remove from pans and transfer onto a wire rack to completely cool.

Flavored Banana Lemon Bread

Prep time: 20 minutes
Cook time: 45 minutes
Servings: 2 loaves

INGREDIENTS

1 cup of chopped walnuts (optional)
1 cup of chocolate chips (optional)
3/4 cup of milk, 2%
3 eggs
1 1/2 cup of sugar
3/4 cup of shortening, butter flavored
2 tbsp of lemon juice
3 (6-8 bananas) cup of bananas, mashed
1 1/2 tsp of cinnamon, ground
1 tsp of baking soda
1 tsp of salt
3 tsp of baking powder
3 1/2 cup of flour, sifted

INSTRUCTIONS

1. Heat the oven to 350 F. Grease 2 loaf pans then sprinkle with flour.
2. In a medium bowl, sift flour, baking soda, cinnamon, baking powder and salt. Set aside.
3. Mash the bananas with fork in a bowl. Stir in the lemon juice until smooth.
4. Cream sugar and shortening into banana mix with an electric mixer; add the eggs and beat well until finely blended.
5. Add the dry ingredients into banana mixture alternately with the milk. Gently fold in the nuts and chocolate chips with a wooden spoon. Pour mixture into the prepared loaf pans.
6. Place pans in the oven and bake for about 45 to 60 minutes. Let cool in pans for about 10 minutes, before transferring to a wire rack to cool completely.

Flatbread With Sausage Marinara Sauce Toppings

Prep Time: 25 minutes
Cook Time: 15 minutes
Servings: 6

INGREDIENTS

6 flatbreads
1/2 (26 oz) of jar marinara sauce
2 teaspoons of Italian seasoning
1 egg
1 (3 oz) package of Parmesan cheese
1 (8 oz) package of shredded mozzarella cheese, divided
1 (15 oz) container of ricotta cheese
1 pound sausage

INSTRUCTIONS

1. Preheat oven to 350 degrees F.
2. Combine 1/2 of the mozzarella cheese, ricotta cheese, Parmesan cheese, Italian seasoning, and egg in a small bowl.
2. Pour sausage into a skillet and cook over medium heat until it's no longer pink, about 5 minutes or more. Drain, then stir in the marinara sauce.
3. Spread the cheese mixture on the flatbread, then the sausage

mixture. Add the reserved mozzarella cheese over the top.
4. Place in preheated oven and bake until cheese melts and bubbly, 10 minutes or more.

Cinnamon Strawberry Bread

Prep Time: 20 minutes
Cook Time: 1 hr
Servings: 8

INGREDIENTS

1 tsp of baking soda
2 Tbsp of canola oil
3 beaten eggs
1 tsp of salt
3 cups of all purpose flour
2 pkg of sliced strawberries, frozen (thaw)
1 Tbsp of cinnamon
2 cups of sugar

INSTRUCTIONS

1. Heat the oven to 350 F.
2. Grease two loaf pans with butter and line each of the pans with foil.
3. Mix the cinnamon, baking soda, flour, salt and sugar together in a large bowl.
4. Create a hole in the center of the flour mixture. Add beaten eggs and canola oil into the hole.
5. Stir everything together until just moistened
6. Add the strawberry slices into a bowl and gently drop them into the mixture using a slotted spoon.
7. Slowly add the juice from the strawberries, stirring until well combined but not too thick.
8. Bake for 60 minutes at 350 degrees or until it's done. Allow to sit in pans for 15 minutes. Run a knife through the edges to loosen the sides of the loaf pan.
Let cool completely, slice.

Filling Banana Marbled Bread

Prep time: 10 minutes
Cook time: 55 minutes
Servings: 8-10

INGREDIENTS
1 tbsp of cinamon sugar (optional)
1/4 cup of crushed toasted walnuts (optional)
1/4 cup of cocoa powder
1/2 tsp of salt
3/4 tsp of baking soda
3/4 cup of sugar
2 cups of flour
1 tsp of vanilla extract
1/4 cup of plain yogurt
2 eggs
6 tbsp room temperature butter
3 ripe bananas

INSTRUCTIONS
1. Heat the oven to 350 F. Grease a loaf pan with cooking spray.
2. In a bowl, mix together the yogurt, butter, and banana. Add in vanilla plus the eggs and blend for 1 minute.
3. Whisk together the flour, baking soda, sugar, and salt in a separate bowl.
4. Add the dry ingredients to the wet ingredients and mix until completely blended. Add in crushed walnuts and mix briefly.
5. Pour about 1/2 to 3/4's batter into the loaf pan.
6. Mix the remaining batter with cocoa powder and mix until blended.
7. Pour the cocoa powder mixture over batter in loaf pan. Swirl the top of batter with a spatula to create a marbled look. Sprinkle with cinnamon sugar.
8. Place loaf pan in the oven and bake for 55 minutes or until a toothpick inserted in the center comes out clean.

VEGETABLES RECIPES

Tomatoes Shallots Convection Roast

Prep time: 30 minutes
Cook time: 4 hours
Servings: 3 cups

INGREDIENTS

1 finely chopped can of anchovies (2 oz drained)
¼ cup of capers (drained)
Freshly ground pepper
¼ cup of extra virgin olive oil
2 large shallots, sliced
5 pounds of tomatoes, peeled and seeded
Salt to taste

INSTRUCTIONS

1. Heat-up the oven to 275 degrees. Line your baking sheet with parchment paper.
2. Toss 2 tablespoon of oil with shallots in a bowl. Spread the shallots evenly on the prepared baking sheet.
3. Add tomatoes with extra oil in the same bowl; season with salt and pepper.
Spread the tomatoes onto the shallots, cut side on top.
4. Bake in the oven for 3 hours. Let cool.
5. Spread shallots with tomatoes in a large tray or bowl along with anchovies and capers.
6. Cover with olive oil and place in the refrigerator overnight. Serve with bread or grilled sandwiches.

Black Bean Cheesy Flautas

Prep time: 20 minutes
Cook time: 20 minutes
Servings: 6

INGREDIENTS

10 (8-inch) whole wheat flour tortillas
Sea salt to taste
1/2 black pepper
1 tsp of chili powder
1 tsp of cumin
1 (4 ounce) can of diced green chiles
1 cup of reduced-fat cheddar cheese, shredded
2 (15-ounce) cans of black beans, drained

INSTRUCTIONS

1. Heat the oven to 325 F. Line your cookie sheet with parchment paper.
2. In a medium mixing bowl, add black beans, green chiles, cheese, chili powder, black pepper, cumin, and salt. Mash the ingredients together using a fork until well blended.
3. Spread the mixture evenly onto the tortillas and roll tightly. Lightly brush each side of tortillas with olive oil or spray with non-stick spray. Place the rolls, seam side down, on the prepared cookie sheet, a few inches apart.
4. Bake in the oven at 350 F for 25 minutes or so, or until the flautas are crispy. Flip halfway through the cooking time. Top with reduced-fat sour cream or fat-free Greek yogurt, if desired.

Note: You can replace 1 tsp of cumin, sea salt, 1 tsp of chili powder, 1/2 black pepper, and 1 tsp of chili powder with 2 tsp of Skinny Ms. Taco Seasoning

Buddha Bowl

Prep time: 30 minutes

Cook time: 30 minutes

Servings: 8

INGREDIENTS

2 firm ripe avocado, diced

1 teaspoon of salt, divided

1 teaspoon of ground pepper, divided

4 tablespoons of tahini

4 tablespoons of water

2 tablespoons of lemon juice

2 15-oz can of chickpeas

6 tablespoons of extra-virgin olive oil, divided

2 small garlic clove, minced

2 medium sweet potatoes, cut into 1-inch chunks

1/2 cup of chopped fresh cilantro or parsley

4 cups of cooked quinoa

INSTRUCTIONS

1. Preheat the oven to 375°F. Blend together the sweet potatoes, half a teaspoon of salt, half a teaspoon of pepper, and two

tablespoons of olive oil in a medium bowl and toss.

2. Transfer the seasoned potatoes to a round baking sheet. Roast and stir briefly until it's soft, about 15 to 18 minutes.

3. Whisk the tahini, garlic, remaining 4 tablespoons oil, water, lemon juice, remaining 1/2 teaspoon salt and 1/2 teaspoon pepper in a small bowl.

4. To serve, divide quinoa among 4 individual bowls. Top with equal parts sweet potato, avocado, and chickpeas. Sprinkle with cilantro or parsley and drizzle with the tahini sauce.

Roasted Green Beans Sweet Onion

Prep time: 5 minutes
Cook time: 45-45 minutes
Servings: 8
INGREDIENTS
2 tbsp of balsamic vinegar
2/3 lbs of green beans
2 tbsp of olive oil
1 lbs of sweet onions, cut into 1/2 size pieces
INSTRUCTIONS
1. Heat up your oven to 350 degrees F.
2. In a large roasting pan, add the onions and drizzle with the oil, toss together to evenly coat.
3. Roast in the oven for 30 minutes, stirring every 8 to 10 minutes.
4. Place the green beans and continue roasting for additional 10 minutes.

5. Pour in the balsamic vinegar and cook about 2 to 5 minutes.

Benny's Potatoes Jive
Prep time: 15 minutes
Cook time: 60 minutes
Servings: 1-4
INGREDIENTS
3 large potatoes, cut into 1/8 inch slices
1/2 tsp of salt
2 Tbsp of parmesan cheese
1 tsp of paprika
1 tsp of garlic powder
1/4 cup of oil
INSTRUCTIONS
1. Heat up the oven to 350 F.
2. Arrange the potatoes slices in a 9 by 13 inch pan in single layers.
3. Combine the remaining ingredients in a bowl and pour over potatoes. Toss to coat.
4. Bake uncovered in the oven for 60 minutes, stirring until brown on both sides.

Roasted Veggies With Lemon And Olives

Prep time: 10 minutes
Cook time: 13 minutes
Servings: 8

INGREDIENTS

2 teaspoons of dried oregano
4 teaspoons of capers rinsed (optional)
20 whole black olives, pitted and sliced
2 tablespoons of extra-virgin olive
2 cups of tomato, grape crowns, trimmed and cut into bite-size florets
4 minced cloves of garlic
2 tablespoons of lemon juice
1/2 teaspoon of salt
4 ounces of broccoli
1 teaspoon of freshly grated lemon zest

INSTRUCTIONS

1. Heat up your oven to 400 degrees F.
2. Blend the tomatoes, garlic, oil, broccoli and salt together in amixing bowl, toss gently until finely coated.
3. Pour the seasoned veggies onto a baking sheet in an even layer, and bake for about 8 to 13 minutes, until the broccoli starts to brown,
4. While the veggies are cooking, combine together the juice, lemon zest, oregano, capers (if using) and olives in a large bowl; stir in the roasted vegetables to combine. Serve while it's warm.

My Special Veggies Turkey Meat Pie

Prep time: 25 minutes
Cook time: 10 minutes
Servings: 6

INGREDIENTS

Toasted sesame seeds, for garnish
2 tbsp of olive oil
6 cups of mashed potatoes
1 tbsp of sesame oil
1/8 cup of soy sauce
4 cups of gravy
1 lbs of leftover turkey meat, boneless, chopped
1/2 cup of dry white wine
1 cup of shelled edamame
1 cup of shiitake mushrooms, sliced in half
4 minced cloves garlic
1/2 cup of diced green onion
1/2 cup of diced onion
1/2 cup of diced celery
1/2 cup of diced carrots
Salt and pepper, to taste

INSTRUCTIONS

1. Heat-up the oven to 450 degrees.
2. Combine all the vegetables in a medium pot and sauté until gently cooked. Add white wine to the vegetables and stir to deglaze; cook until the alcohol smell is no longer strong.
3. Gently fold in the chopped turkey and add the soy sauce, sesame oil and gravy. Taste and adjust seasoning, if necessary.
4. Pour the mixture into a 12 by 8-inch baking dish. Spread the mashed potatoes evenly on top. For a more crispy pie, run a fork over the top to create more grooves. If desired, dot with butter.
5. Place in the oven and bake for 30 minutes. Let it sit for at least 15 minutes before serving. If you prefer it crispier, broil to get your desired crispiness.

Crispy Roasted Broccoli With Garlic

Prep time: 10 minutes
Cook time: 15 minutes
Servings: 4
INGREDIENTS
25 grams of finely grated Parmesan
35 grams of panko bread crumbs
1/4 tsp of freshly ground black pepper
1/2 tsp of salt
2 minced cloves garlic
30 ml of olive oil
500 grams of broccoli, rinsed and trimmed
INSTRUCTIONS
1. Heat the oven to 385 F.
2. Cut the broccoli florets into small pieces. Chop the broccoli stalk into round slices of about 0.5-cm thick.
3. In a mixing bowl, toss the broccoli and with garlic, olive oil, pepper, and salt. set aside.
4. Add the bread crumbs into a non-stick 33 by 23-cm cake pan, and spread evenly. Toast the bread crumbs for 2 minutes in the oven

until lightly toasted.
5. Withdraw the toasted bread crumbs from the oven and place in the bowl. Add the broccoli mixture and toss to combine.
6. Spread mixture in the cake pan, and roast in the oven for 8 to 10 minutes just until the broccoli is tender.
7. Withdraw from the oven, add cheese and serve right away.

Root Vegetable Roast

Prep time: 15 minutes
Cook time: 30-35 minutes
Servings: 4-6

INGREDIENTS

2 tsp of Italian seasoning
2 shallots peeled and chopped
2 medium beets peeled and chopped
4 carrots peeled and chopped
3 cups of turnips peeled and chopped
2 tbsp of olive oil
1/2 tsp of salt

INSTRUCTIONS

1. Heat the oven to 400°F.
2. Add the oil, carrots, turnips, shallots and beets in a large bowl. Toss to coat.
3. Pour veggies into a 9x13 baking dish and spread evenly.
4. Bake for 30-35 minutes in the oven, or until the vegetables are fork tender. Serve with roasted chicken pieces.

Coated Rosemary Mixture Vegetables Toast

Prep time: 20 minutes
Cook time: 35 minutes
Servings: 7

INGREDIENTS

1 tbsp of chopped fresh rosemary
1/4 cup of olive oil
Half small eggplant, cut in quarter and chopped into 1/2-inch
Salt and pepper to taste
1 tbsp of dried oregano
1 red bell pepper, slice in 1/2-inch strips
1 1/2 lbs of new potatoes, quartered
3 tbsp of lemon juice
1 small onion, chopped into wedges
1/2 cup of baby carrots
3 minced cloves garlic

INSTRUCTIONS

1. Heat-up the oven to 450 F.
2. In a 13x9 inch baking pan, mix together potatoes, onion and carrots.
3. In a small mixing bowl, combine oregano, rosemary, garlic, lemon juice, olive oil, salt and pepper. Spread the rosemary mixture on top of the vegetables.
4. Place the baking pan in the heated oven and bake for 20 minutes.
5. Once the 20 minutes is complete, remove pan from oven; add bell pepper and chopped eggplant. Toss to coat everything together.
6. Bake for another 13 to 15 minutes, or until the vegetables are brown and soft.

BEEF PORKS AND LAMB RECIPES

BBQ Sauce Cheesy Meatloaf

Prep time: 15 minutes
Cook time: 1 hour
Servings: 8

INGREDIENTS

1 Tbsp of worcestershire sauce
1 cup of barbecue sauce, divided
1 large sweet chopped onion
2 eggs
2 cups of shredded cheese
1 cup of bread crumbs
2 pounds of ground beef
1/2 tsp of pepper
3/4 tsp of salt

INSTRUCTIONS

1. Heat the oven to 350°F
2. Sauté the onion in a saucepan for about 5 minutes or until lightly browned.
3. Gently mix together the sautéed onion, bread crumbs, meat, eggs, worcestershire sauce, half cup of barbeque sauce, salt, and pepper with your hands until thoroughly mixed.
4. Shape the mixture into a loaf and place it on a large, 2-inch deep baking sheet.
5. Spread the remaining barbeque sauce over the loaves.
6. Bake in the oven for 60 to 75 minutes, or until set. Let it stand for 10 minutes in the baking dish. Slice and serve.

Italian Mustard Pork Chops

Prep time: 5 minutes
Cook time: 10 minutes
Servings: 4

INGREDIENTS

1/2 cup of shredded parmesan cheese
Salt and pepper to taste
6 ounces of pork center loin, boneless (4 each)
1/2 tsp of italian seasoning (mccormick)
1 Tbsp of olive oil, extra virgin
1 Tbsp of dijon mustard

INSTRUCTIONS

1. Heat the oven to 400 degrees.
2. Whisk the Italian Seasoning with mustard in small bowl. Season pork with salt and pepper to taste.
3. Brush the pork with the mixture all over. Press the cheese into the chops on both sides.
4. Transfer onto a parchment paper-lined baking sheet. Bake in the oven for about 8–10 minutes or until it's done. Brush the chops generously with mustard mixture to keep them moist. Let it rest about 5 minutes before serving.

Honey Ketchup Meat Loaf

Prep time: 15 minutes
Cook time: 1 hr 10 minutes
Servings: 6

INGREDIENTS

Cooking spray
1 1/2 pounds of ground round
1 whole egg
1/4 tsp of pepper
1/4 tsp of salt
1 tbsp of brown sugar
2 tbsp of chopped fresh parsley
1/4 cup of minced fresh onion
1/2 cup quick oats
3/4 cup of ketchup, divided

INSTRUCTIONS

1. Preheat the oven to 350°F. Spray a broiler pan with cooking spray.
2. In a large bowl, combine the oats, 1/2 cup of ketchup, egg, onion, parsley, pepper, sugar and salt. Add meat and blend well.
3. Mold mixture into an 8 x 4-inch loaf size on the prepared pan. Brush the meat loaf with 1/4 cup of ketchup.
4. Bake for 1 hour and 10 minutes at 350 F. Remove from the oven and let sit for about 10 minutes before serving.

Onion, Sage Meatloaf

Prep time: 20 minutes
Cook time: 1 hr
Servings: 8-10

INGREDIENTS
1/8 tsp of pepper
1/2 tsp of sage, ground
1 tsp of salt
2 eggs, beaten
1/4 cup of onion, chopped
2/3 cup of bread crumbs
1 cup of milk
1 1/2 pounds of ground beef or turkey

TOPPING
1 tbsp of dry mustard
1/4 tsp of nutmeg
3 tbsp of brown sugar
1/4 cup of ketchup

INSTRUCTIONS
1. Heat the oven to 350 F. Spray the loaf pan with non-stick cooking spray.
2. Pour milk into a mixing bowl, and soak bread crumbs in milk.
3. In another bowl, whisk together the eggs, meat, onion, sage, salt and pepper with the soaked crumbs and mix.
4. Mix the dry mustard, ketchup, nutmeg, and brown sugar in separate bowl.
5. Add the meat mixture into loaf pan, spread evenly, and spread the ketchup mixture over the top.
6. Bake for 50 to 60 minutes. Remove from the oven and let sit for about 10 minutes before serving. Serve over mashed potatoes or rice.

Skewed Meatball Kebobs

Prep time: 15 minutes
Cook time: 15 minutes
Servings: 4

INGREDIENTS

Skewers
1 cup of favorite barbecue sauce or more
1 medium onion, cut into chunks
1 red pepper, cut into chunks
1 yellow or green pepper or both, cut into chunks (you can also use squash)
24 cooked meatballs let it come to room temperature

INSTRUCTIONS

1. Heat-up the oven bake 375 degrees F. Line a cookie sheet pan with foil.
2. Pierce a skewer through a piece of onion, meatballs, green pepper, a second meatball, followed by a red pepper, and then alternate using different vegetables. Follow the same process until you have pierced about 4-6 meatballs into the skewer, ending with onion pieces. Repeat.
3. Brush the skewered balls on both sides with BBQ sauce and place meatballs on the prepared cookie sheet pan.
4. Bake about 15-20 minutes at 375 degrees until veggies are crisp tender and balls are heated through.

Vegetable Beef Slow Roast

Prep time: 15 minutes
Cook time: 6-8 hrs
Servings:

INGREDIENTS

1 can of water
1 can of cream of mushroom soup
1 onion soup mix
Sliced onions
Sliced bell pepper
Sliced carrots
1 quartered potatoes
1 beef roast
Salt and black pepper

INSTRUCTIONS

1. Heat the oven to 200 degrees F.
2. Add the beef roast in a foil lined 9 X 13 X 2-inch baking pan. Place the vegetables all around the roast.

3. Add onions, cream of mushroom soup, soup mix and water to the pan; Season with salt and black pepper. Wrap with foil.
4. Place in the oven and bake for 6 - 8 hours at 200 degrees F.

Roast Pork Tenderloin

Prep time: 20 minutes
Cook time: 1 hrs 15 minutes
Servings: 6-8

INGREDIENTS

2 cup of hot water
1 (10 3/4 ounce) can of cream of mushroom soup
1 package of Lipton onion soup mix
1-2 Tbsp of olive oil
1/2 cup of flour
1/8 tsp of pepper
(Optional) 1/2 tsp of salt
2 1/2 pounds of pork tenderloin, Trim off as much fat as you can

INSTRUCTIONS

1. Heat up the oven to 375 F.
2. Season both sides of the pork tenderloin with salt and pepper.
3. Dip tenderloin in flour and roll to coat well.
4. Heat olive oil over medium heat in a cast-iron skillet. Add the tenderloin and brown it on all sides.
5. In a mixing bowl, mix together hot water, mushroom soup, and onion soups mix.
6. Slowly add the soup mixture to the roast. Try and allow the onion pieces to rest over the tenderloin as much as you can.
7. Cover and bake in the oven for about 75 minutes, or until it is done and it reads 170 degrees in the inner temperature.

Ground Beef Tomatoes Jalo Nachos

Prep time: 20 minutes
Cook time: 15 minutes
Servings: 3

INGREDIENTS

1 tbsp of chili powder
1 tbsp of garlic powder
Sour cream for topping
1 chopped green bell pepper
1 chopped onion
1 diced tomatoes
Lettuce, shredded
2 chopped Jalapenos
1 cup of cheddar cheese
1 bag of tortilla chips
1 lb of ground beef

INSTRUCTIONS

1. Heat the oven to 350 F.
2. Heat the oil in a pan over medium heat; add the beef and brown it, stirring with a wooden spatula.
3. Add the chili powder, pepper, garlic powder, and salt, and cook stirring to mix well.
4. Add the bell peppers and chopped onion and mix thoroughly. Continue cooking for 10 to 15 minutes until the vegetables are soft.
5. Spread the tortilla on the baking sheet, and top with beef/veggie mix, jalapenos and cheese.
6. Place in the oven and bake for 10 minutes at 350 F.

8. Remove pan from the oven, and top with sour cream, tomatoes, and shredded lettuce.

Apple Onion Pork Loin

Prep time: 30 minutes
Cook time: 2 hours30 minutes
Servings: 6

INGREDIENTS

Salt and freshly grounded pepper to taste
1/3 cup of water
1-2 tablespoons of butter
2-3 large onions, sliced
8-10 apples, peeled and sliced
4 pounds of pork loin, boneless
1-2 tablespoons of oil

INSTRUCTIONS

1. Heat-up the oven to 350 F.
2. Score the pork loin in multiple places to allow heat penetrate the meat, and then transfer to a roasting pan.
3. Pour about 1-2 tablespoons of oil into the pan and brown pork on all sides.
4. Drain any residual liquid from cooking; add butter to pan, onions, apples, and water.
5. Cover and bake for approximately 2 hours. Uncover and continue baking for 1/2 hour (adding a few drops of water if it seems too dry). Season with salt and pepper.

Serve with egg noodles or buttered band noodles.

Soft Horseradish Rib Roast

Prep time: 20 minutes
Cook time: 45 minutes
INGREDIENTS
1 1/2 tsp of freshly ground black pepper
1 tbsp of salt
1 (7 to 8 pounds) beef standing rib roast (3-rib) (Allow the meat to thaw for two hours before roasting)
For the Sauce
1 1/2 tbsp of whole-grain mustard
1/3 cup of sour cream
1 tbsp of prepared horseradish
3 tbsp of Dijon mustard
1 1/2 cups of good mayonnaise
1/4 tsp of salt
INSTRUCTIONS
1. Heat the oven to 430 F.
2. Place the oven rack in the second lowest position in the oven.
3. Place the roast bone-side down in a pan, large enough to hold the meat, and season the top freely with pepper and salt.
4. Roast uncovered for about 50 minutes, reduce to 325 F and continue roasting for additional 30 minutes.
5. Increase oven temperature to 430 F and let it roast for extra 15 to 30 minutes. It should read 122 F when a thermometer is inserted in the center of the roast. The total cooking time will be between 1 1/2 and 1 3/4 hours.
6. Meanwhile, in a small bowl, whisk together the mustards, sour cream, horseradish, mayonnaise, and salt.
7. Once the roast is done, remove from the oven and place on a cutting board covered in aluminum foil tightly for about 20 minutes. Carve and serve with the sauce.

SEAFOOD RECIPES

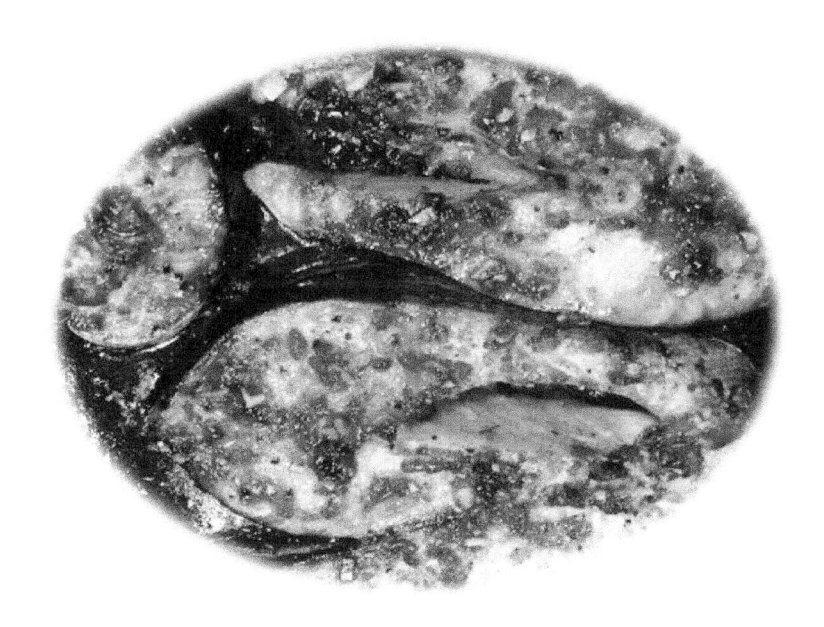

Perfect Cooked Salmon Fillet

Prep time: 10 minutes
Cook time: 20 minutes
Servings: 8-10

INGREDIENTS

3/4 tsp of pepper
1 tsp of salt
3 minced cloves garlic
3 tbsp of olive oil (or canola)
6 tbsp of lemon juice
4 lbs of fresh salmon fillet (Rinse and pat dry)

INSTRUCTIONS

1. Heat up the oven to 400 F.
2. Cut a large piece of aluminum foil and wrap it around the entire fillet, positioning the salmon fillet skin side down on the foil. Transfer to a shallow pan or baking sheet.
3. Mix the oil, lemon juice, pepper, garlic, and salt together in a small bowl and pour over the fillet in the pan.
4. Wrap fish in foil, sealing the edges but give room for expansion.
5. Bake in the oven for 10 minutes. Then cook each inch of fish thickness for 10 minutes or until fish easily flakes with a fork.
6. Remove fish from oven, remove foil and discard skin. Serve with Basil-Cilantro Sauce or Mustard Sauce, or Creamy Dill.

Soy Miso Sake-Glazed Salmon

Prep time: 10 minutes
Cook time: 5 minutes
Servings: 4

INGREDIENTS

4 (5 to 6 ounces each) skinless salmon filets, cut in 1 inch thick
1/4 cup of sugar
2 tbsp of vegetable oil
1 tbsp of soy sauce
1/3 cup of sake
1/4 cup of red or white miso

INSTRUCTIONS

1. Whisk the soy sauce, oil, sake, miso, and sugar together in a bowl. Season the salmon filets thoroughly with the mixture.
2. Place the salmon filets in a sealable container or plastic zip lock bag. Marinate for about 30 minutes or 48 hours. (If you are in a rush, proceed to the next step).
3. Preheat the oven's broiler on high. Cover a small oven-roaster broiling pan with aluminum foil. Dust off any excess marinade from the fish and transfer to the broiling pan.
4. Broil for about 5 minutes or until salmon is heated in the center and surface is well charred. Protect any areas that are likely to get burnt with foil. Serve and enjoy.

Convection Broiled Lobster Tails

Prep time: 10 minutes
Cook time: 10 minutes
Servings: 2

INGREDIENTS

1 tsp of lemon pepper seasoning
1 tbsp of olive oil
2 (6 oz.) of frozen lobster tails, thaw partially

INSTRUCTIONS

1. Cut the lobster tail shells open lengthwise, down the back, using kitchen scissors.
2. Brush the inner part of the meat lightly with olive oil and season with lemon pepper.
3. Place on oven roaster broiling pan with the cut side facing up.
4. Place about 6 inches from the heat source and broil for about 10 minutes, or until they are slightly browned at the edges and opaque.

Coconut Crackers Crispy Tilapia

Prep time: 10 minutes
Cook time: 15 minutes
Servings: 6

INGREDIENTS

6 (4 ounce) tilapia fillets
1/3 cup of liquid egg whites
1/4 cup of Whole Wheat Ritz crackers (crushed)
1/4 cup of Italian bread crumbs
1/4 cup of shredded coconut

INSTRUCTIONS

1. Heat- up the oven to 375 F. Line your baking pan with foil and spray with cooking spray.
2. Combine crackers, bread crumbs, and coconut in a bowl.
3. Add the egg whites in a separate bowl.
4. Run fish in the egg whites, then coat in the coconut mixture.
5. Arrange tilapia fillets on the prepared baking pan.

6. Bake at 375 F for 15-20 minutes, or until tilapia is done. (Check for doneness after 15 minutes.)

Gouda Magic Shrimp Scampi

Prep Time: 45 minutes
Cook Time: 1h 10 minutes
Servings: 12

INGREDIENTS

2 teaspoons salt
4 tablespoons of butter or margarine
16 ounces smoked Gouda, grated
1/2 cup heavy cream
4 eggs
3 (8 oz) packages cream cheese, softened
12 shells of puff pastry, baked
1 pound of fresh shrimp, peeled and deveined
6 teaspoons of minced garlic
1 onion
1 tablespoon of olive oil

INSTRUCTIONS

1. Preheat oven to 325 degrees F.
2. Heat the oil in a large skillet over medium-low heat. Add the garlic and onions, and sauté until the onions are translucent. Allow the liquid to cool before pouring it off.
3. Cut the shrimp into 1/2 inch pieces, leaving 12 whole (for garnish). Melt butter in a large skillet over medium-low heat. Add the shrimp and the reserved garlic; cook for 3 to 4 minutes.
3. Remove the puff pastry shell's center circle and a small cool portion inside.
4. Beat cream cheese in a medium bowl until creamy. Beat in one single egg at a time until thoroughly mixed. Add Gouda, shrimp, onions, salt, and cream.
5. Add the filling into the puff pastry shells with spoon.
6. Place in the preheated oven and bake until the filling top is browned. About 20 to 25 minutes. Garnish with chopped chives and the reserved 12 whole shrimp.

Spicy Teriyaki Worcester Salmon

Prep time: 5 minutes
Cook time: 30-40 minutes
Servings: 6

INGREDIENTS

Juice from 1/2 lemon
(Optional) 1/2 stem lemongrass, chopped or crushed
1 pinch of ground pepper
1 pinch of himalayan salt
2 large grated garlic cloves
2 tbsp of ginger grated
1 tbsp of Indonesian sweet soy sauce
1/2 tbsp of worcester sauce
2 tbsp of teriyaki sauce
4 tbsp of tamari soy sauce
4 tbsp of sweet chili sauce
6 good-sized salmon fillets

INSTRUCTIONS

1. Heat the oven to 356 F.
2. On a flat plate, season the fish fillets with a little of salt and set aside.
3. Combine the Worcester sauce, fish sauce, teriyaki sauce, tamari soy sauce, Indonesian sweet soy sauce, lemongrass, freshly grated ginger, sweet chilly, lemon juice, freshly ground pepper, and freshly grated garlic in a bowl. Mix well.
4. Dip each salmon fillet in the sauce and make sure all sides are well coated in the sauce. Transfer to the baking tray.
5. Scoop or brush any remaining sauce over the salmon fillets in the tray.
6. Bake in the oven for about 30-40 minutes until it's done.

Convection Oven Prawns

Prep time: 15 minutes
Cook time: 10 minutes
Servings: 4

INGREDIENTS

1/3 cup of coriander (leaves finely chopped)
1/4 cup of soy sauce
1 Tbsp of olive oil
1 tsp of sesame oil
2 minced garlic cloves
Juice of 1 lemon
35 ounces of medium raw shrimp (prawns peeled and deveined)

INSTRUCTIONS

1. In a small bowl, combine the olive oil, garlic, lemon juice, sesame oil, coriander, and soy sauce.
2. Add prawns in a ceramic or glass dish, and pour in the marinade; toss to coat everything together. Cover and place the pan in the refrigerator for 30 minutes.
3. Heat the oven to 180° C.
4. Place marinated prawns in a baking dish, cover with foil and bake in the oven until cooked through, about 10 minute.
Serve with broccolini, rice, and snow peas (steamed).

Halibut In Mushroom Sherry Sauce

Prep time: 15 minutes
Cook time: 30 minutes
Servings: 4

INGREDIENTS

4 (1 1/2 pounds total) of halibut fillets
2 tbsp of melted butter
Salt to taste
Black pepper to taste

For the Sauce:

1/4 tsp of garlic seasoned pepper
1/2 tsp of seasoned salt
1 tbsp of sherry
1 cup of milk
1/2 cup of chicken broth
3 tbsp of flour
4 to 6 thinly sliced green onions
4 to 6 ounces of sliced mushrooms
3 tbsp of butter

INSTRUCTIONS

1. Preheat the oven to 325 F. Grease your baking dish with butter.
2. Arrange the halibut fillets in the prepared baking dish.
3. Brush fillets with melted butter and season with pepper and salt.
4. Bake in the preheated oven for 20 to 25 minutes until the fish begins to flake easily with a fork, basting periodically with the melted butter. Once its done, remove and let cool for 5 minutes.
5. Melt butter over medium-low heat in a saucepan, and add the mushrooms. Cook, stirring constantly until mushrooms are tender and golden brown. Add the sliced onions and cook for 1 minute more, stirring. Add in flour and stir until finely blended. Cook for 1 extra minute.
6. Slowly stir in milk and broth until mixture is smooth. Add seasonings along with the sherry. Cook, stirring frequently until the sauce is bubbly and thickened.

Serve fish on a serving plate with the sauce.

Easy Flakes Halibut With Scallop And Shrimp

Prep time: 10 minutes

Cook time: 8-12 minutes

Servings: 2

INGREDIENTS

1 tbsp of fresh chopped parsley

Salt and pepper to taste

1 tsp of minced garlic

1/2 tsp of Old Bay seasoning

1 tbsp of lemon juice

2 tbsp of melted butter

1/3 cup of dry white wine

6 jumbo shrimp, peeled and deveined, tail still attached

6 scallops

2 (4 ounce) of halibut fillets

INSTRUCTIONS

1. Heat the oven to 425 F.
2. In an oven-safe glass baking dish, place the shrimp, halibut, and scallops. Drizzle with melted butter, wine, and lemon juice. Sprinkle with minced garlic, seasoning, salt and pepper.
3. Bake for 10 to 12 minutes in the oven until the fish flakes easily and has turned white. Serve garnished with fresh chopped parsley.

White Cod Fillet Gondola

Prep time: 15 minutes
Cook time: 25 minutes
Servings: 1

INGREDIENTS

1 tsp of olive oil
Salt and pepper
1 bread stick
1 lime, cut in half
1 Tbsp of lemon pepper
4 baby new potatoes, thin sliced
1 carrot, thin sliced
2 cabbage leaves, shredded
1 medium white cod fillet

INSTRUCTIONS

1. Heat the oven at 350°F. Season the cod fillet with salt, lemon pepper, and pepper.
2. Place the cabbage on a large piece of aluminum foil, add cod fillet, then brush fish with the olive oil on top. Place the potatoes and carrot over the fish.
3. Wrap fish in foil over and then compress the ends so it looks like a gondola.
4. Bake in the over at 350°F for 25 to 35 minutes. Remove from oven and transfer to a plate, place the bread stick and lime beside it. Unwrap and dig in!

Orange Fennel Fish Fillet

Prep time: 10 minutes
Cook time: 45 minutes
Servings: 8

INGREDIENTS

2 tablespoon of grated orange peel
1 teaspoon crushed thyme, dried
1 teaspoon crushed oregano, dried
2 teaspoon of crushed fennel seed
6 tablespoon crushed basil, dried
1/2 cup orange juice
2 cup dry white wine
2 pounds fillet of sole fish
2 minced garlic clove
1/2 cup lemon juice
32 ounce of canned tomatoes, drained, coarsely chopped (juice reserve)
2 large sliced onion
4 teaspoon of olive oil
2 bay leaves

INSTRUCTIONS

1. Heat the olive oil in large nonstick pan, sauté the onion in the pan over medium heat until the onion is tender and brown slightly, for 5 minutes.
2. Set the fish aside and pour in the remaining ingredients. Stir and simmer without covering for 30 minutes.
3. Arrange fish in a baking dish. Pour the sauce on top and bake without covering for about 12-15 minutes, at 325 F or until fish easily flakes.

POULTRY AND CHICKEN RECIPES

Convection Chicken Wings

Prep time: 4 minutes
Cook time: 16 minutes
Servings: 4
INGREDIENTS
1 teaspoon of lemon pepper
2 teaspoons of garlic salt
1 tablespoon of olive oil
1 pounds of chicken wings split into flats and drummettes
INSTRUCTIONS
1. Pat chicken dry on paper towels and transfer into a bowl.
2. Drizzle 1 tablespoon of oil on the chicken wings. Sprinkle with 1 teaspoon of lemon pepper and 2 teaspoons of garlic salt on top. Toss to coat.
3. Place coated chicken in a baking pan. Bake for 8-12 minutes per side at 400°F, or until chicken wings are golden brown and crispy.

Tomatoes Baby Spinach Chicken Casseroles

Prep time: 20 minutes
Cook time: 35 minutes
Servings: 2 casseroles (5 servings each)
INGREDIENTS
2 cups of Colby-Monterey Jack cheese, shredded
3 cups of fresh baby spinach, chopped
4 medium tomatoes, seeded and chopped
1 cup of mayonnaise
1 cup of 2% milk
1 cup of crumbled cooked bacon
2 (10-3/4 ounces each) cans of condensed cheddar cheese soup, undiluted
4 cups of cooked chicken, cubed
4 cups of uncooked spiral pasta
INSTRUCTIONS
1. Heat the oven to 350 F. Cook pasta as directed in the

package instructions. Drain.
2. Combine together the condensed cheddar cheese soup, mayonnaise, chicken cubes, milk and bacon in a large bowl. Gently stir in the spinach and tomatoes.
3. Stir pasta into the chicken mixture and pour the mixture into 2 greased 8-inch square baking dishes. Sprinkle top with shredded cheese.
4. Bake in the oven for 30-40 minutes or until cheese is melted and bubbly.

Turkey Oats Meatloaf

Prep time: 25 minutes
Cook time: 30 minutes
Servings: 8
INGREDIENTS
2 lbs of lean ground turkey
1/4 tsp of pepper
1 tsp of garlic powder
2 tbsp of ketchup
1/4 cup of egg substitute
1/2 cup fat-free milk
1/2 cup of carrots, shredded
1 medium onion, chopped
1 cup of quick-cooking oats
TOPPING:
1/4 cup of quick-cooking oats
1/4 cup of ketchup
INSTRUCTIONS
1. Heat the oven to 325 F. Grease a 9x5-inch loaf pan with cooking spray.
2. Combine the oats, garlic powder, milk, carrots, onion, egg substitute, ketchup, and pepper in a mixing bowl. Add the turkey; lightly mix until thoroughly coated.
3. Mix together the quick-cooking oats and ketchup in a bowl.
4. Pour oat mixture into the prepared pan and then add the carrot mixture on the top loaf.
5. Bake in the oven for 55-65 minutes or until a thermometer

inserted in the center reads 165°. Leave to stand for 10 minutes before slicing.

Chicken Double Cheddar & Rice Bam
Prep time: 10 minutes
Cook time: 35 mis
Servings: 6
INGREDIENTS
1/3 cup of Italian bread crumbs
2 cups of shredded cheese
2 box rice a roni creamy four cheese rice
1 jar of ragu double cheddar sauce
6 chicken breasts
INSTRUCTIONS
1. Cook rice as directed in box directions.
2. Meanwhile, you either fry or bake the chicken until it's done. Set aside.
3. Once the rice is cooked, mix in 1/2 cheddar sauce and make sure it's well mixed.
4. Transfer rice mix to baking dish, use a spatula to spread and place cooked chicken over top in a single layer

Chicken_Bebita

Prep time: 30 minutes
Cook time: 45 minutes
Servings: 5

INGREDIENTS

1 tbsp of mustard
Pepper to season chicken
Salt to season chicken
1/2 tbsp of goya seasoning
1/2 tbsp of paprika
1 1/2 cup of bread crumbs, seasoned
10 chicken, drumsticks
1 can of coconut milk

INSTRUCTIONS

1. In a 1-gallon ziplock bag, combine the mustard, paprika and coconut milk. Seal the bag and mix thoroughly. Add chicken to bag and set aside for 30 minutes.
2. Preheat the oven to 400°F. Once the 30 minutes is complete, add Goya seasoning (or favorite seasoning) and bread crumbs to a plate
3. Season drumsticks with pepper and salt and then roll in bread crumbs mixture until completely covered completely.
4. Place drumsticks on a baking sheet and bake in the oven for 45 minutes.

Spaghetti Chicken Casserole

Prep time: 25 minutes
Cook time: 35 minutes
Servings: 8

INGREDIENTS

1 1/2 cup of broken tortillas strips
3 cup of cheddar cheese, shredded
1 large jar of salsa with white corn and black beans
1 can 8 ounces of tomato sauce
1/2 cup can of yellow corn, drained
1/2 cup can of black beans, drained
1 pkg of fajita seasoning
1 small onion, diced
1 medium green bell pepper, diced
1 bag of fajita chicken, cut into pieces
16 ounces of spaghetti

INSTRUCTIONS

1. Cook pasta as directed in package directions. Drain and set aside.
2. Add 1 tbsp. olive oil in a large skillet. Sauté the onions, green bell peppers, and chicken pieces. Add the fajia seasoning to the skillet, and sauté for 5 minutes.
3. Add black beans, salsa, corn and tomato sauce, stir and simmer for 5 minutes.
4. Heat the oven to 350 F.
5. Pour 1/3 of the bean mixture into a lightly sprayed casserole dish. Add half the pasta, and add 1/3 of bean mixture. Add 1 cup of cheese and the remaining pasta, add 1 extra cup of cheese, and lastly the remaining 1/3 bean mixture.
6. Place in the oven and bake at 350 F 25 minutes. Top with last cup of cheese and tortillas 5 minutes to final baking time.

Chang Chicken Casserole

Prep time: 15 minutes

Cook time: 60 minutes

Servings: 4

INGREDIENTS

1 Tbsp of hot sauce

2 Tbsp of teriyaki sauce

2 Tbsp of flour

1 Tbsp of worcestershire sauce

2 Tbsp of vinegar

3 Tbsp of brown sugar

4 Tbsp of soy sauce

3/4 tsp of garlic powder

1 pound of chicken breast, chopped

6 chopped celery stalks

1 medium chopped bell pepper
1 medium chopped onion

INSTRUCTIONS

1. Heat the oven to 425 F. Smear a square casserole dish with non-stick spray
2. Combine the chicken breast, bell pepper, celery, and onion together in the dish, and sprinkle with garlic powder.
3. In a bowl, combine the remaining ingredients and mix until well blended. Pour the mixture over the chicken.
4. Cover the casserole dish with foil and bake at 425 F for 60 minutes. Serve over rice.

Roasted Chicken Breast With Prosciutto Green Beans

Prep time: 5 minutes
Cook time: 25 minutes
Servings: 2

INGREDIENTS

2 wedge lemon
6 thinly slices prosciutto
2 skinless boneless chicken breast half
Coarse salt and ground pepper
4 tsp of olive oil
8 ounces of green beans

INSTRUCTIONS

1. Heat the oven broiler to high. Toss 1 teaspoon of oil with the green beans in the pan; season with pepper and salt. Gather the green beans towards one side of pan.
2. Season chicken breast with grounded pepper and salt, then wrap in prosciutto.
3. Place the wrapped chicken, seam side down, in the pan with the green beans; rub with the remaining olive oil.

4. Place in the oven and broil for 15 to 20 minutes, or until the chicken is opaque throughout. Serve green beans and chicken along with a lemon wedge.

Cheez-it Tender Chicken

Prep time: 20 minutes
Cook time: 15 minutes
Servings: 8
INGREDIENTS
2 pounds of chicken tenders pounded out
1 1/2 cups of buttermilk
1 whisked egg
Few dashes hot sauce
1-2 cups of crushed cheeze-its
Olive oil
1/4 tsp dried dill
INSTRUCTIONS
1. Preheat the oven to 425 degrees F.
1. Start by pounding the chicken tenders.
2. In a medium mixing bowl, combine the eggs, milk, hot

pepper sauce, and butter.
3. Soak chicken in milk/ egg, mixture and refrigerate for 60 minutes.
4. Meanwhile, crush 1/4 tsp of dried dill with cheez-its in the food processor. Transfer to a large platter.
5. Once the 60 minutes is complete, drain the chicken and coat well in cheeze-its mix.
6. Transfer chicken to a large baking sheet and drizzle with oil.
7. Bake in the oven at 425 at degrees for 7 minutes, turn over and bake for extra 7-9 minutes until golden brown. Serve with your favorite dipping sauce.

Noodle Mushroom Chicken Casserole

Prep time: 20 minutes
Cook time: 45 minutes
Servings: 6
INGREDIENTS
1 stick of real butter
1 pkg of ritz crackers: crushed
1/2 cup of chicken broth
2 bouillon cubes
1 tsp of salt and pepper
1 pkg of egg noodles
8 ounces of sour cream
1 can of cream of mushroom soup
1 can of cream of chicken soup
4-5 large chicken breasts
INSTRUCTIONS
1. Heat the oven to 350 F. Generously spray an 8 x 12 Pyrex baking dish with cooking spray.
2. Bring a large pot of water to a simmer. Add the chicken breast, 2 bouillon cubes, salt, and pepper. Cook for about 20 minutes until the chicken is done. Remove chicken. Scoop out 1 cup of cooking liquid. Allow to cool.
3. Cook the egg noodles in the same pot as the chicken until

they are tender. Drain and set aside.

4. Cut the cooked chicken into bite-sized chunks, and transfer them into a large bowl. Mix in sour cream, cream of chicken soup, cream of mushroom soup and salt and pepper to taste. Add in the noodles and mix to blend. Add a little reserved broth.

5. Pour the mixture into the prepared baking dish. Sprinkle top with cracker crumbs and spread melted butter over the crackers.

6. Place the baking dish in the oven and bake for 45 minutes or until bubbly.

Cream Cheese Worcestershire Chicken Breast

Prep time: 15 minutes
Cook time: 30 minutes
Serving: 4
INGREDIENTS
Toasted bread crumbs
1/2 cup of melted butter
2 dashes of garlic powder
2 tablespoons of plum jam
Dash of Worcestershire
8 ounces of cream cheese
4 chicken breasts (boneless)
INSTRUCTIONS

1. Pound chicken flat and thin using a rolling pin inside a gallon zip-top bag. Sprinkle with half dash garlic powder, salt, and pepper.

2. Mix together the remaining half dash of garlic powder, softened cream cheese, Worcestershire, and plum jam. Spread mixture evenly over chicken. Roll jelly-roll fashion.

3. Pour the melted butter and toasted bread crumbs in different bowls. Coat each chicken breast in butter, remove and coat in the bread crumbs.

4. Bake the chicken for 30 to 35 minutes at 350°F. Do not over bake so the chicken won't become tough.

Tasty Buffalo Wings

Prep time: 15 minutes
Cook time: 45 minutes
Servings: 24

INGREDIENTS

1/4 tsp of sea salt
1/2- 1 1/2 tsp of red pepper sauce
1 Tbsp of vinegar
3 Tbsp of butter, unsalted
1/4 cup of all purpose flour
2 pounds of chicken wings, cut from joints to give you 3 pieces, discard tip
Blue cheese dressing

1. Remove and discard any excess skin from the chicken wing. Heat up the oven to 425 F.
2. In a 13-9-2 inches rectangular pan, heat 2 tablespoons of the butter until melted.
3. Add flour to a mixing bowl. Coat the chicken pieces in flour, and shake off any excess flour on the chicken. Place coated chicken in pan
4. Bake for 20 minutes without covering, flip and bake for extra 20 to 25 minutes. Drain.
5. Melt the last tablespoon of butter and combine it with the pepper sauce, vinegar, and salt in a mixing bowl. Add wings and toss to coat. Serve chicken with blue cheese dressing.

Chicken Mini Chimichangas

Prep time: 15 minutes
Cook time: 15 minutes
Servings: 8

INGREDIENTS

1 cup of cooked rice
1 cup of shredded chedder or jack cheese
1/4 cup of melted butter
8 flour tortillas 7 - 8 inches
1/2 tsp of salt
1/2 tsp of oregano leaves
1/4 tsp of ground cumin
1/3 cup of green onion sliced
2/3 cup of salsa, mild
2 1/2 cup of shredded chicken cooked

INSTRUCTIONS

1. Combine cooked rice, shredded chicken, onion, salsa, oregano leaves, cumin and salt in a saucepan. Simmer for about 5 minutes, or until most of the liquid has evaporated.
2. Brush one side of the tortilla with melted butter. Over the center of the unbuttered side, spoon about 1/3 cup of the chicken mixture.
3. Add 2 teaspoons of cheese to the top. Fold the buttered sides on top of the filling, then fold the ends down.
4. Place the tortilla filling, seam side down, in a 13 x 9 baking dish.
5. Bake for 13 minutes at 475 degrees in a preheated oven or until crisp. Add guacamole and salsa on top.

Walnut Honey Chicken Breast

Prep time: 5 minutes
Cook time: 30 minutes
Servings: 3-4
INGREDIENTS
Salt & pepper to taste
1 cup of ground walnuts
1 1/2-2 cup of bread crumbs
1 cup of honey
1 1/2-2 pounds of boneless chicken breasts
INSTRUCTIONS
1. Pour the honey into small bowls. Combine walnuts and bread crumbs in separate small bowls. Dip chicken breast in honey, remove and roll in bread crumb/walnuts mixture.
2. Season the coated chicken with salt and pepper to taste. Chill for about 60 minutes in the refrigerator.
3. Bake in the oven for 45 minutes at 350 degrees or until it's done.

Roasted Duck With White Vermouth And shallot

Prep time: 10 minutes
Cook time: 3 hours minutes
Servings: 4

INGREDIENTS
For the duck
Half yellow onion, cut in half
1/2 orange, cut into quarters
2 (5" long) fresh rosemary sprigs
Freshly ground black pepper to taste
Kosher salt to taste
1 5- to 6 pound of duck
For the sauce
Freshly ground black pepper
Kosher salt
1/2 teaspoon of finely grated orange zest
1/2 teaspoon of chopped fresh rosemary
3 to 4 tablespoons of unsalted butter, softened
1/2 cup of unsalted chicken stock
1 cup of dry white vermouth
3 tablespoons of minced shallot

INSTRUCTIONS
1. Heat the oven to 325°F degrees and place a rack in the center.
2. Remove the tips of the duck's wings and any giblets if you wish. (They can be used as parts for stock if desired.)
3. Trim the duck of any excess fat and skin and rinse well. Season the duck generously with salt and pepper.
4. Stuff the onion, rosemary, and orange into the duck's cavity. Secure the duck's two legs with kitchen twine.
5. Arrange the duck in a heavy-duty roasting pan with the breast side up.
6. Place pan in the oven, and roast for about 3 hours or until it the crispy, browned, and tender. Set aside on a carving board.
7. Drain the duck dripping from the pan but reserve a few teaspoons. Add the shallot and cook over medium heat, stirring for 2 to 3 minutes until softened but not browned.

8. Stir in chicken stock and vermouth, and deglaze. Turn the heat up and boil on high for 5 to 7 minutes until the liquid is reduced to about 2/3 cup.
9. Turn heat off, and remove the pan. Then add butter and whisk vigorously, one tablespoon at a time.
10. Strain sauce into a vessel through a fine-mesh strainer. Whisk in orange zest and rosemary, and season with pepper and salt to taste. Carve duck with a knife and pour sauce over the duck.

Tender Cooked Duck With Currant Jelly Glazed

Prep time: 10 minutes
Cook time: 60 minutes
Servings:
INGREDIENTS
1 Tbsp of currant jelly
1 tsp of lemon juice
2 cup of orange juice
1/4 tsp of ginger
1/2 tsp of paprika
1/2 tsp of pepper
1 tsp of salt
1 wild duck,
INSTRUCTIONS
1. Heat the oven to 400 F.
2. Mix the ginger, salt, paprika, and pepper in a bowl. Rub the mixture thoroughly on duck.
3. Place the seasoned duck in a roasting pan, and bake for 60 minutes at 400 degrees F. Drain off fat.
4. Meanwhile, mix together currant jelly, lemon juice, and orange juice, and pour over the duck. Baste constantly as you keep baking until tender.

Chicken Ham Schnitzel Cordon Bleu

Prep time: 20 minutes
Cook time: 20 minutes
Servings: 2

INGREDIENTS

1 tbsp of melted butter
1 tbsp of canola oil
1/2 cup of seasoned bread crumbs
2 tbsp of 2% milk
1 large egg
1/8 tsp of pepper
1/8 tsp of paprika
1/4 tsp of salt
1/2 cup of all-purpose flour
2 (3/4 ounce each) Swiss cheese slices
2 (3/4 ounce each) deli ham slices
2 (6 ounces each) boneless skinless chicken breast, cut in halves

INSTRUCTIONS

1. Pound the chicken into 1/4-inch thick; Place a slice of ham and cheese on top of each chicken. Roll up the chicken and fold the ends in. Keep them secured with toothpicks.
2. Combine together the flour, paprika, pepper and salt in a shallow bowl.
3. Whisk together the milk and egg in another bowl.
4. In a third bowl, place the bread crumbs.
5. Coat the chicken in the flour mixture, then in the egg mixture, and finally in the bread crumbs.
6. Heat oil in a small skillet and brown the chicken on all sides.
7. Spray a square baking dish with cooking spray, place the chicken in it, and bake for 20-25 minutes at 325°F, or until a thermometer reads 170°.

Remove toothpicks and drizzle with butter.

APPERTIZERS AND SNACKS RECIPES

French Toast Pumpkin Walnuts Casserole

Prep time: 480 minutes
Cook time: 55 minutes
Serving: 4

INGREDIENTS

1/2 cup of milk
1/3 cup of butter, cold/sliced
1/2 cup of Walnuts
1/2 cup of brown sugar
4 cups of French loaf, or any other bread, diced
1/2 cup of pumpkin puree
Pinch of nutmeg powder
1/4 tsp of cloves, ground
1-1/2 tsp of cinnamon powder
Salt to taste
2 tbsp of sugar
1 tsp of vanilla extract
2 whole eggs

INSTRUCTIONS

1. Whisk together the eggs, pumpkin puree, brown sugar, sugar, salt, ground cinnamon, ground cloves, ground nutmeg, and vanilla extract in a medium bowl just until combined. Do not over-mix. Add in the milk and stir again.
2. Brush some butter on an 8 x 8 baking dish. Distribute the diced bread evenly in the pan. Pour the mixture on top of the bread, making sure it's well covered.
3. Stir together with a spatula to coat. Cover the baking dish with plastic wrap, and place in the refrigerator overnight.
4. Preheat oven to 180 C. Remove the baking dish from the refrigerator and discard the plastic wrap. Top with slices of butter all over and spread walnuts on top.
5. Place in the oven and bake without covering, for 40 to 45 minutes, or until it's set and the knife inserted in the center comes out dry. Let cool for ten minutes before serving.

Browned Oven Crispy Granola

Prep time: 10 minutes
Cook time: 45 minutes
Servings: 5

INGREDIENTS

1/2 tsp of vanilla
2 tbsp of walnut oil or coconut oil
1 tbsp of honey
2 tbsp of maple syrup
3 scant tbsp of light brown sugar
1 medium egg white, lightly beaten
3/8 tsp of salt
2 tsp of toasted wheat germ
Optional 1/4 cup of walnuts or 1/4 cup extra oats
1/2 cup of pecans
1/2 cup of slivered almonds
1 1/2 cups of rolled oats

INSTRUCTIONS

1. Heat-up the oven to 275F.
2. Stir the almonds, rolled oats, walnuts, wheat germ and pecans together in a large bowl. Add salt and stir.
3. Spread the beaten egg white over the almond/oat mixture, and stir to combine.
4. Combine the oil, maple syrup, honey, and brown sugar together in a heat-proof cup and microwave for about 1 minute on high. Stir to dissolve the sugar. Stir in vanilla.
5. Spread the sugar mixture on top granola and stir to coat evenly.
6. Spread the oat mixture evenly onto two heavy and large cookie sheets lined with parchment paper; press down slightly to create a thin, closely packed layer of oats.
7. Bake in the oven for 35 to 45 minutes, stirring every 15 minutes, until the granola is nicely browned and crisp when you remove it from the oven.

Jumbo Jet Shells

Prep time: 20 minutes
Cook time: 22 minutes
Servings: 3-4

INGREDIENTS

1/2 cup of grated Parmesan cheese
1/2 (about 3 ounces) bag of fresh spinach
1 (24 ounces) jar of marinara sauce
2 lbs of ricotta cheese
1 (12 ounces) pkt of dry pasta jumbo shells
2 tbsp of olive oil
8x8-inch baking pan

INSTRUCTIONS

Preheat the oven to 375°F,

1. Cook the pasta jumbo shells according to package instructions. Grease your baking pan with the oil.
2. Stuff ricotta cheese inside each cooked shell and place them in the prepared pan, cheese-side up.
3. Stir the spinach and marinara sauce together in a bowl. Spread mixture over stuffed shells.
4. Place pan in the oven and bake for 20 minutes. Remove the pan from the oven and sprinkle the tops of the shells with parmesan cheese.
5. Place the pan in the oven and broil for 2 minutes.

Brie Cheese Apricot Puffed Pastry

Prep Time: 10 minutes
Cook Time: 30 minutes
Servings: 8

INGREDIENTS

1 egg white
1 (8 oz) wheel of Brie cheese
3 tablespoons of apricot preserves
1/2 (17.5 oz) of package frozen puff pastry, thawed

INSTRUCTIONS

1. Preheat oven to 325 degrees F. Grease a cookie sheet lightly.
2. Divide one wheel of Brie cheese into two circles of cheese. Spread one side of the half circle of brie with apricot preserves and lay the other circles of brie on the apricot preserves to form a sandwich.
3. Wrap a sheet of puffed pastry over the whole wheel of Brie and place it onto the earlier prepared cooking sheet, setting the seam on the bottom. Brush the egg white on the puffed pastry.
3. Place in the preheated oven and bake until the pastry is golden brown, about 30 minutes. Serve immediately.

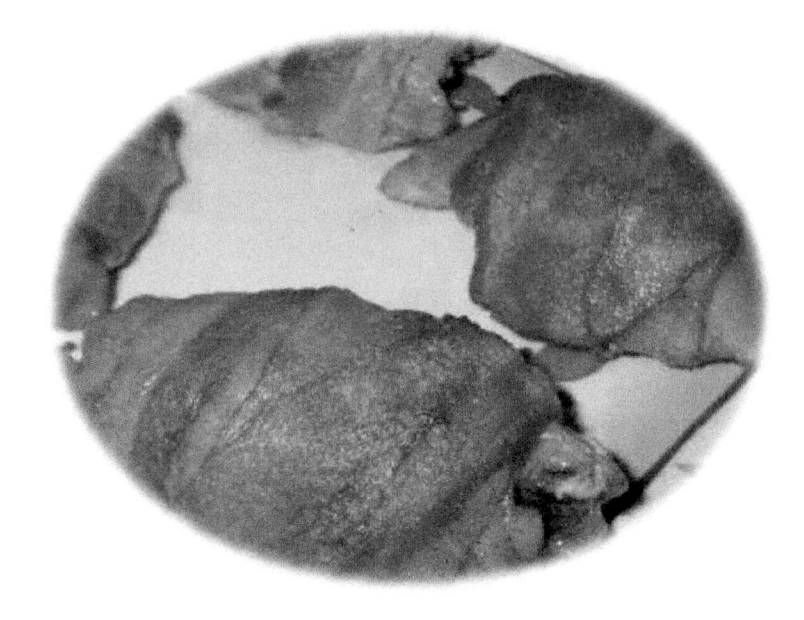

Cinnamon Smokies Wraps

Prep time: 25 minutes
Cook time: 20 minutes
Servings: 32

INGREDIENTS

1 small bag of Bryan cocktail smokies; 12 ounces
1 can of cinnamon rolls, 8 counts

INSTRUCTIONS

1. Heat the oven to 350 F. Lightly spray a cookie sheet with cooking spray.
2. Prepare the cinnamon rolls by cutting each into four long pieces with a pizza cutter and flatten them with your hand.
3. Wrap the cinnamon roll around each smokie.
4. Place each of the cookie sheet-wrapped smokies in the prepared cookie sheet with a few inches apart.
5. Place the cookie sheet in the oven and bake for 20 minutes or until brown. Remove and transfer to a serving plate.

Cheesy Ginger Chili Bread

Prep time: 10 minutes
Cook time: 30 minutes
Serving: 4

INGREDIENTS

Butter, for brushing
Salt and Pepper, to taste
2 tsp of Red Chilli flakes
2 tbsp of finely chopped coriander leaves
2 tbsp of finely chopped mint leaves
1 tsp of grated Ginger
200 grams of grated Homemade Cottage Cheese
10 slices of Whole Wheat Brown Bread

INSTRUCTIONS

1. Cut off the brown edges from the bread. Gently roll the bread slices with a rolling pin. Set aside.
2. Heat up the oven to 180 c.
3. Combine together chilli flakes, ginger, grated cottage cheese, coriander, mint, salt, and pepper in a mixing bowl. Mix until thoroughly combined. Set aside.

To prepare the bread rolls

4. Spoon one tablespoon of the mixture over one rolled bread slice, a little bit towards one of the edges. Use a little water to brush the other edges to help seal the roll. Carefully seal the edges tightly to make a roll. Repeat these steps for other bread rolls.
5. Arrange bread rolls on a baking sheet and brush with melted butter all over.
6. Place tray in the oven and bake at 180 c for 12 to 15 minutes or until golden. Remove tray from oven. Serve with tomato sauce or Spicy & Creamy Chicken Gravy.

Bacon Chicken Thighs

Prep time: 10 minutes
Cook time: 1 hour 25 minutes
Servings: 4

INGREDIENTS

4 chicken thighs
8 smoked bacon slices
2 tbsp of dried tarragon
Pinch of salt
Pinch of black pepper
Pinch of garlic salt
Tsp of paprika

INSTRUCTIONS

1. Season the chicken thighs with dried tarragon, garlic salt, paprika, pepper, and salt.
2. Wrap chicken thighs with 2 slices of smoky bacon. Transfer to a baking pan and cover with foil.
3. Bake in the oven for 50-60 minutes at 350 degrees. Open and discard the foil and increase the oven temperature to 400 degrees. Bake for extra 20–25 minutes or until bacon is brown. Drain off fat.

Merry Bells Pizzas

Prep time: 5 minutes
Cook time: 10 minutes
Servings: 2

INGREDIENTS

Pinch of basil or parsley
Pinch of red pepper flakes
1/2 cup of grated cheese
1/2 cup of spaghetti sauce or pizza sauce
2 large bell peppers
Toppings of choice (such as broccoli and tomatoes)

INSTRUCTIONS

1. Heat-up the oven to 350 F.
2. Cut off the peppers from all four sides and place them flat on the baking sheet.
3. Top with spaghetti sauce or pizza sauce, grated cheese, and desired toppings.
4. Bake in the oven for 10 minutes, turning over to oven broil towards the final baking time for a nice and bubbly cheese.

Add a pinch of basil or parsley and red pepper flakes if desired.

Convection Baked Gnocchi Alfredo

Prep time: 5 minutes
Cook time: 17 minutes
Servings: 4-6

INGREDIENTS

5 fresh basil leaves, cut in strips, for garnish
1/2 cup of Parmesan cheese, shredded
1 (14 ounces) jar of alfredo sauce
1/4 cup of vegetable stock
2 (24 ounces total) bags of frozen potato gnocchi

INSTRUCTIONS

1. Evenly spread frozen gnocchi onto the baking pan, then pour the vegetable stock over gnocchi. Preheat the oven to 390°F.
2. Arrange the baking pan in the oven and bake for 12 minutes at 390°F. Once you are 10 minutes into the baking time, remove pan from the oven, stir well with a spatula or wooden spoon. Place it back in the oven and continue baking for 2 minutes more.
3. Withdraw baking pan from the oven, evenly spread the alfredo sauce on top of the gnocchi, and stir well to coat. Sprinkle top with Parmesan cheese.
4. Place baking pan in the oven and broil for about 3-5 minutes or until lightly browned on top and cheese is melted.
5. Remove pan from oven and serve in serving dish, decorate with basil.

Spaghetti Beef Lasagna Rolls

Prep time: 25 minutes
Cook time: 10 minutes
Servings: 6

INGREDIENTS

2 cups of part-skim mozzarella cheese, shredded, divided
(Optional) 1/2-1 tsp of fennel seed
1 (14 ounces) jar spaghetti sauce
1 lbs of ground beef
6 lasagna noodles

INSTRUCTIONS

1. Cook the lasagna noodles as directed in the package instructions. Drain.
2. Meanwhile, cook the ground beef in a large skillet over medium heat until it's no more pink; drain. Stir in half of the spaghetti sauce and fennel seed, if using. Cook until thoroughly heated.
3. Pour 1/4 cup of sauce mixture on top of each noodle; sprinkle top with 2 tbsp. of mozzarella cheese.
4. Gently roll up the noodles, and transfer them into an 8-inches square baking pan with the seam side down. Spread the remaining half of the sauce on top, along with the remaining cheese.
5. Bake in the oven for 10-15 minutes at 375 F, or until cooked through and cheese is melted.

DESSERT RECIPES

Peach Lemon Pies

Prep time: 30 minutes
Cook time: 20 minutes
Servings: 8

INGREDIENTS

Cooking spray
1 (14.1-ounces) pkg. of refrigerated piecrusts
1 tsp of cornstarch
1/4 tsp of salt
1 tsp of vanilla extract
3 tbsp of granulated sugar
1 tbsp of fresh lemon juice (from 1 lemon)
2 (5-ounces) of fresh peaches, peeled and chopped

INSTRUCTIONS

1. Stir the lemon juice, vanilla, peaches, sugar, and salt together in a medium bowl. Set aside and let stand for 15 minutes, stirring periodically. Drain but reserve one tbsp. liquid. Whisk together reserved liquid and cornstarch; stir into drained peaches. 2. Cut piecrusts into eight circles (about 4-inch). Fill the center of the piecrusts with 1 tablespoon of the peach filling.
3. Brush dough edges with water; then fold in half forming half-moons. Seal dough edges with a fork. Make 3 small cuts in the top pies and coat the pies thoroughly with the cooking spray.
4. Arrange pies in the oven and bake for 12 to 14 minutes at 350°F until golden brown.

Amazing Peanut Butter Cookies

Prep Time: 30 minutes
Cook Time: 10 minutes
Servings: 36

INGREDIENTS

2 teaspoons of baking soda
1 teaspoon of vanilla extract
1 pinch of salt
2 cups of white sugar
2 cups of peanut butter
2 eggs

INSTRUCTIONS

1. Heat the oven to 325 degrees F. Brush cookie sheets with grease.
2. Add the sugar and peanut butter together in a medium bowl; stir until smooth. Whisk in the eggs one after another. Mix in the vanilla, salt, and baking soda.
3. Mould the dough into 1-inch patties and place them on the prepared sheet. Lay the cookies 2 inches apart from each other and use the back of a fork to Press a criss-cross on the cookies.
4. Place the cookies in the oven and bake for 8 to 10 minutes. Leave to cool for 5 minutes, then transfer it to a wire rack to completely cool.

Churros With Chocolate Cream Sauce

Prep time: 50 minutes
Cook time: 30 minutes
Servings: 12

INGREDIENTS
2 tbsp of vanilla kefir
3 tbsp of heavy cream
4 oz of bittersweet baking chocolate, finely chopped
2 tsp of ground cinnamon
1/3 cup of granulated sugar
2 large eggs
1/2 cup of all-purpose flour (about 2 1/8 oz.)
1/4 cup of unsalted butter, divided plus 2 tablespoons
1/4 tsp of kosher salt
1/2 cup of water

INSTRUCTIONS
1. Bring water, a quarter cup of butter, and salt to a boil in a small saucepan over medium-high heat. Reduce the heat to low-medium.
2. Add in the flour, stirring thoroughly using a wooden spatula for about 30 seconds until you have a smooth dough. Cook, stirring frequently, for about 2 to 3 minutes until it forms a film on the bottom of the pan and dough starts to pull away from pan sides.
3. Place dough in a bowl, stirring constantly for about 1 minute until it cools a bit.
4. Crack the egg and add it to the dough (one at a time), stirring frequently after each addition until totally blended. Pour the mixture into a pastry bag with a fitted medium star tip. Set aside to chill for 30 minutes.
5. in a single layer, pipe the mixture into 3-inch long pieces in 6 places in the baking pan. Bake for about 10 minutes at 380°F until golden. Repeat.
6. In a medium bowl, stir together cinnamon and sugar. Use the remaining 2 tbsp. of melted butter to brush the cooked churros, and coat them in the sugar/cinnamon mixture.
7. Microwave cream and chocolate on high in a small

microwave-safe bowl, for about 30 seconds, stopping to stir after 15 seconds. Add kefir and stir. Serve churros alongside the chocolate sauce.

Best Dessert Cake

Prep time: 20 minutes
Cook time: 30 minutes
Servings: 9 inch double-layer

INGREDIENTS

4 egg whites
1 tsp of vanilla
1 1/4 cup of milk
2/3 cup of vegetable shortening
1 tsp of salt
4 tsp of baking powder
1 1/2 cup of sugar
2-2/3 cup of cake flour, sifted

INSTRUCTIONS

1. Grease the base of two 9, plus 1 half-round layer cake pans and line with wax paper. Grease wax paper and flour on the surface.
2. In a large bowl, mix together the flour, baking powder, vanilla, sugar, 3/4 cups of milk, shortening and salt.
3. Beat with an electric mixer on low speed until well combined, then beat for two additional minutes at high speed. Add the egg whites with the remaining half cup of milk; beat for 2 extra minutes at high speed. Scrape down the sides of the bowl as necessary.
4. Transfer the batter to the cake pans. Bake for 30 minutes at 350 degrees, or until the toothpick inserted into the center comes out clean.
5. Remove the pan from the oven and let it cool on wire racks for 10 minutes, run a knife around the edges to loosen it. Invert onto wire racks and discard waxed paper.
6. Allow to cool completely, then fill the desiredcake and frost to your desire.

Stylist Monkey Bread

Prep time: 5 minutes
Cook time: 30 minutes
Servings:

INGREDIENTS

10-count refrigerator biscuits, cut into 1/4
2 tbsp of granulated sugar
2 tbsp of brown sugar
1/2 tsp of cinnamon
2 tbsp of melted butter, (plus more for greasing the ramekin)
1/2 cup of diced apples

TOPPING

1/2 tsp of cinnamon
1 tbsp of brown sugar
1 tbsp of butter, melted

INSTRUCTIONS

1. Heat- up the oven to 350 F.
2. Roll each 1/4 biscuit into small balls. Set aside.
3. In a small bowl, mix together the cinnamon and sugars and pour them into a small ziplock bag.
4. Roll each dough ball in melted butter and place it into a ziplock bag. Seal the bag and shake until the balls are coated completely.
5. Grease the ramekin generously.
6. Layer coated dough balls onto the bottom of the ramekin, and layer with diced apples.
7. Layer another dough over the apples.
8. Mix together the cinnamon, melted butter and brown sugar in a small bowl.
9. Pour the cinnamon/butter mixture on top of the dough.
10. Bake for 25-30 minutes in the oven, until slightly browned on top. Withdraw from the oven and set aside for 2-3 minutes to cool. Invert onto a plate.

Vanilla Peanut Butter Cookies

Prep time: 5 minutes
Cook time: 15 minutes
Servings: 30

INGREDIENTS

1 tsp of vanilla
1 egg
1 cup of sugar
1 cup of peanut butter

INSTRUCTIONS

1. Heat the oven to 325 F.
2. In a mixing bowl, mix together the entire ingredients thoroughly.
3. Line a baking sheet with parchment paper and drop the mixture by teaspoonfuls with two inches apart.
4. Press the cookie with a glass bottom dipped in sugar.
5. Bake in the oven for about 14 to 16 minutes or until lightly browned. Allow cooling on rack.

Easy Roasted Figs

Prep time: 15 minutes
Cook time: 10 minutes
Servings: 4

INGREDIENTS

Cinnamon powder
4 tsp of Honey
80g Marscapone
4 Fresh Figs

INSTRUCTIONS

1. Cut the fig into almost a quarter, stopping at the base so it can hold together.
2. Grease an oven tray with 1 tsp of oil. Place the quartered figs over the prepared tray, then drizzle 1 tsp of honey over each fig.
3. Dollop 2 teaspoons of marscapone in the center of each fig, then sprinkle the marscapone generously with cinnamon.

4. Place the tray in the oven and bake for 10 minutes. Quickly pour the caramelized honey on top of each before it hardens. Serve hot or cold.

Lemon Cake Cookies

Prep Time: 15 minutes
Cook Time: 15 minutes
Servings: 36
INGREDIENTS
1/3 cup of confectioners' sugar
1 teaspoon of lemon extract
1/3 cup of vegetable oil
1 (18.25 oz) package of lemon cake mix
2 eggs
INSTRUCTIONS
1. Preheat oven to 350 degrees F.
2. Pour the lemon cake mix into a medium bowl. Stir in lemon extract, oil, and eggs. Blend until smooth.
3. Drop dough by teaspoonfuls into confectioners' sugar in a bowl. Roll here and there until they are a bit covered. Place on an ungreased cookie sheet.
4. Place in the preheated oven, and bake for 7 minutes, or more until the inside becomes chewy and light brown at the bottom

Convection Toaster Brownies

Prep time: 15 minutes
Cook time: 45 minutes
Servings: 16

INGREDIENTS

1/2 cup of fair trade chocolate chips
1/2 tsp of vanilla
2 eggs
1/2 cup of melted butter
3/4 cup of granulated sugar
1/3 cup of fair-trade unsweetened cocoa powder
1/2 tsp of salt
1/2 tsp of baking powder
Half cup of all-purpose flour plus 2 tablespoons
8×8 baking pan

INSTRUCTIONS

1. Heat the oven to 325 F. Grease the 8 x 8 baking pan thoroughly.
2. Combine together the cocoa powder, flour, baking powder, sugar, and salt in a medium bowl until well blended.
3. In another small bowl, blend the eggs, vanilla, and butter with a fork until well blended.

4. Add milk/egg mixture to cocoa/flour mixture and stir until just incorporated. Add the chocolate chips, stir.

5. Pour mixture into greased baking pan, place pan in the oven and bake for 35 to 45 minutes, turning once halfway through baking until a toothpick you insert into the brownies 2 inches from the edge comes out with a few crumbs. Allow to cool on a wire rack in the pan before slicing and serving.

Oatmeal Raisin Cookies

Prep time: 10 minutes
Cook time: 15-20 minutes

INGREDIENTS

1 cup of raisins
1 tsp of ground cinnamon
1 tsp of baking soda
1/3 cup of sugar
1 cup of brown sugar
1 tsp of vanilla
1 cup of butter
1/2 tsp of salt
2 eggs
1 cup of flour
2 1/2 cups of uncooked quick Oats or old fashioned

INSTRUCTIONS

1. Preheat the oven 350°F
1. In a big bowl, mix together the vanilla, butter, salt, and brown sugar.
2. Mix in the eggs, ground cinnamon, baking soda, and sugar until well blended. 3. Mix in the flour thoroughly. Stir in the Oats and mix until well blended. Add raisins and mix.
4. Place a spoonful of the mixture onto a cookie sheet (ungreased) (about six per batch). Press down to flatten.
5. Bake in the oven for 15-20 minutes at 350°F or until brown at the top.

Printed in Great Britain
by Amazon